MORE THAN 400 AMAZING COLOR PHOTOS THROUGHOUT THE BOOK!

NATIONAL GEOGRAPHIC KiDS

ULTIMATE BUG-OPEDIA

BY DARLYNE MURAWSKI & NANCY HONOVICH

THE MOST COMPLETE BUG REFERENCE EVER

NATIONAL GEOGRAPHIC
WASHINGTON, D.C.

CONTENTS

COMPLETE METAMORPHOSIS 132

Coleoptera – **Beetles**

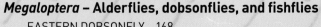

Megaloptera – **Alderflies, dobsonflies, and fishflies**

Neuroptera – **Lacewings and antlions**

Hymenoptera – **Ants, bees, sawflies, and wasps**

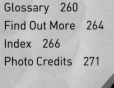

Siphonaptera – **Fleas**

Diptera – **Flies**

Trichoptera – **Caddisflies**

Lepidoptera – **Butterflies and moths**

MORE ABOUT BUGS 248

INTRODUCTION

Insects are endlessly fascinating. They come in many sizes, shapes, and colors. They walk, fly, jump, swim, and burrow. They eat many things—and many things eat them. As they grow, they often transform themselves from one shape into a very different one. A few are harmful to us, but overall we need insects for many reasons—and, in fact, we need them for our own survival.

As an entomologist, my job is to study insects. I find something surprising about every insect that I encounter.

The *Ultimate Bugopedia* beautifully illustrates the diversity that scientists have discovered about insects and how they live. With more than 80 profiles of individual insects of different species and with many insect gallery spreads of even more insects within a group, along with hundreds of color photos throughout, this is a book that speaks to the life of insects. How do the bright colors of butterflies protect them from being eaten? Why do fireflies make their bodies flash? You'll find the answers to these questions and to just about anything else you want to know about insects in this book.

With *Bugopedia* as your guide and inspiration, you can go to your backyard, or almost anywhere, to study insects on your own. Observe insects carefully, and you can make your very own scientific discoveries about them.

When I was young, no single book encompassed the diversity of insect life like this one does. So you are lucky. With *Bugopedia* as your companion, I hope that you will discover the world of insects and become as fascinated with it as I am.

Bill Lamp, Ph.D.

Welcome to the *Ultimate Bugopedia*—a big source for information on the fascinating world of insects, with more than 400 photos. Insects are the most abundant and successful group of animals on earth—with more than a million known species and many more yet to be discovered. As a scientist and as a writer, I enjoyed working on this book, and I hope you will enjoy reading it.

When I was a child, I loved observing "bugs" and exploring nature outdoors. Those times provided endless small discoveries for me—like how bees visited different flowers in our garden at different times of day and how butterflies would try to stick their proboscises in the center of each flower on my brightly colored shirt!

My early enthusiasm for insects started me on a path toward pursuing my interests in a big way. As an adult, I've been fortunate to work as a biologist who studies butterflies and plants, and as a nature photographer who photographs them. In my travels around the world to places like Thailand, India, and the Amazon region of South America, I've encountered countless insects with amazing adaptations for survival. You can see a few of my photos of them on this page.

You may find yourself with a similar fascination for insects and their relatives. Some of the insects profiled in this book will be familiar to you, and others won't. The insects you'll see are from various parts of the world, and each has a story to tell. Enjoy exploring *Bugopedia*. You'll find another great thing about insects is that you never have to outgrow your interest in them. I haven't.

Darlyne Murawski, Ph.D.

HOW TO USE THIS BOOK

Bugopedia is filled with information about insects.

Here you will find a guide to some of the pages in the different sections.

The first section, "Discovering Bugs," is an introduction to everything about these amazing animals. It will help you learn about and understand them, so that when you read the profiles of individual species, you'll already be in the know. The "Life Cycle of an Insect" is one topic explored in this section.

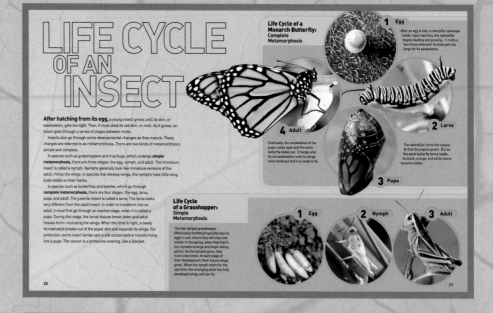

The second and third sections, the largest parts of the book, feature profiles of different insect species. They are organized by the type of metamorphosis that the insects undergo: simple or complete. The insects are then further arranged by their groups or orders. The pages at the right show insect orders for complete metamorphosis.

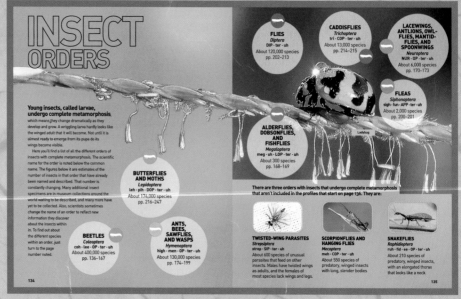

There are eighty-three individual profiles of insect species in the book. Here is an example of one of them.

GOLDEN TORTOISE BEETLE

FAMILY CHRYSOMELIDAE

Tortoise beetles look like they have an upside-down bowl over their backs, legs, and head. The bowl is actually their front wings and part of their thorax. It protects them so that predators, like ants, can't grab hold of them.

The golden tortoise beetle is named for its golden, jewel-like appearance on morning glory leaves, their preferred food. However, the bug isn't always golden. It can change its colors. The color change depends on the amount of fluids between layers inside their wings. The fluid is controlled by microscopic valves.

This color change once fooled scientists into believing that they were observing different species of beetles, not one. They even gave the beetle different names.

The larvae of the golden tortoise beetle have an effective way of defending themselves. They have a long, forklike extension at the end of their abdomen that holds large gobs of feces. When they hold this extension (called a fecal parasol) over their bodies, predators ignore them.

FACTS

OTHER COMMON NAME	Sweet potato leaf beetle		
SCIENTIFIC NAME	*Charidotella sexpunctata* / Family: Chrysomelidae	SIZE	0.20–0.28 inch (5–7 mm) long
WINGS	Yes (their forewings are hardened wing covers and their hind wings are for flying)		

HABITAT	Found on morning glories
RANGE	North America

138   139

Throughout the book, there are photo galleries—ten in all—that will show you even more species within a group than the ones individually profiled. The butterflies gallery below is one example.

BUTTERFLIES GALLERY

Butterflies have amazing wings made up of thousands of tiny scales. These scales can be brightly colored or dull, and even transparent. Some butterflies have shiny, metallic colors, like the morpho.

Butterflies use their wing colors and patterns in many ways. They can be used for camouflage, to absorb heat, and to find a mate. Some toxic butterflies also rely on their bright colors to warn predators that they taste foul. Potential enemies, like birds, learn to keep away. With about 20,000 butterfly species, these fluttering insects live just about anywhere in the world. They can be found in rain forests, mountaintops, deserts, cities, and even your own backyard. Do you have a favorite of the species shown here?

A Malayan zebra butterfly drinks from moist, rocky soil. In Southeast Asia, these butterflies are often seen mud-puddling with other butterflies.

The peacock butterfly lives in Europe and parts of Asia. Its flashy eyespots may help deter predation. Adult butterflies hibernates over the winter.

Cairns birdwing is Australia's largest native butterfly. It inhabits the rain forests of Queensland on the northeast coast.

A small skipper butterfly rests at attention on a flower stalk. Skippers have strong wing muscles for darting in flight.

A close-up of a butterfly's iridescent wing scales. The optically formed colors that you see depend on the angle at which you look at the wings.

This cattleheart butterfly from Jamaica is a type of swallowtail butterfly. Its fuzzy thorax is covered in tightly packed black and red hairs.

232   233

DISCOVERING BUGS

A sweet potato bug laying her eggs

A river jewelwing damselfly

Southern green stink bugs newly hatched from their eggs

Tree nymph butterfly

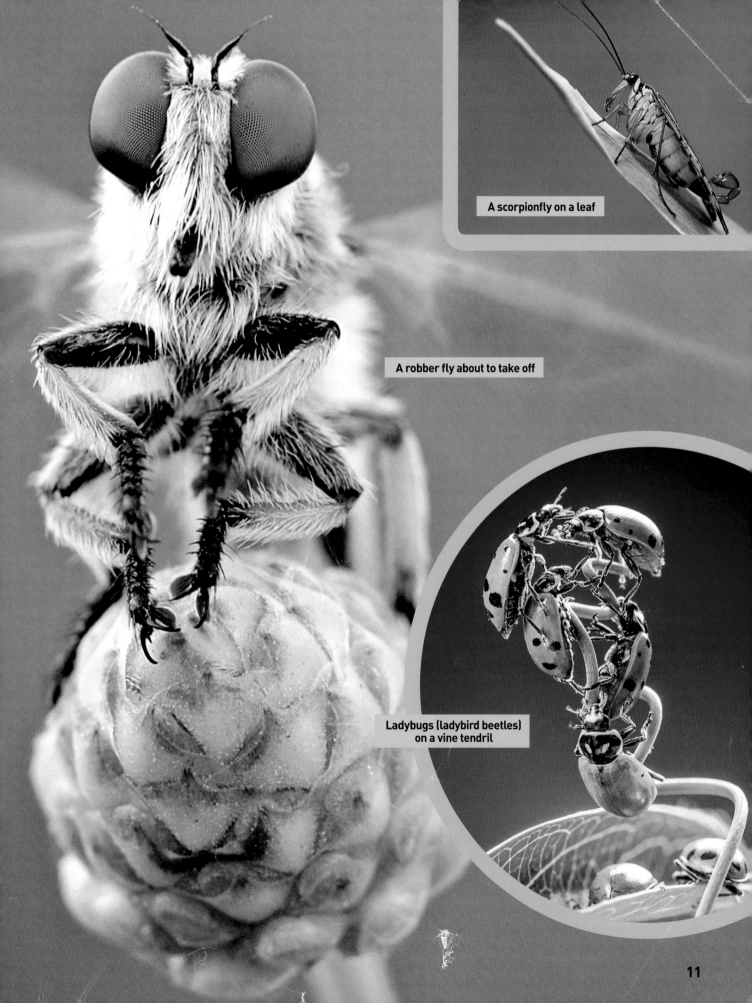

A scorpionfly on a leaf

A robber fly about to take off

Ladybugs (ladybird beetles) on a vine tendril

WHAT IS A BUG?

Look around you. It's not hard to find bugs. They crop up just about anywhere. But let's start off by thinking about what a bug actually is. To many, a bug is any small critter that looks vaguely like an insect, spider, or worm. To an entomologist, a scientist who studies insects, a bug refers to a specific group of insects called "true bugs." But generally, and in this book, the word "bug" is used to mean "insect." Not all of what we sometimes think of as bugs are insects, though: spiders and worms, for instance, aren't insects.

Insects have a hard external skeleton, called an exoskeleton. They have no spine, like we have. Along with other spineless animals, they are called invertebrates. Invertebrates also include spiders, worms, jellyfish, sponges, snails, crabs, and octopuses. Of all the invertebrates, insects are the only ones that evolved wings.

All insects have certain features in common. They have three main body sections: the head, thorax, and abdomen. On its head, an insect has eyes and two antennae. Insects have compound and simple eyes, although some have lost one or the other. On its thorax, an adult insect has six legs and two pairs of wings. Beyond these common features, insects have differences, such as types of mouthparts, wings, and shape of antennae, that separate them into various groups.

HIND WING

ABDOMEN

COMPOUND EYES

SIMPLE EYES

This cicada has two large compound eyes and three small, pink simple eyes.

SCIENTIFIC CLASSIFICATION OF THE DRAGONFLY

Scientists divide animals into groups to help our understanding. Here's how the dragonfly gets grouped.

Kingdom: Animalia (animals)

Phylum: Arthropoda (jointed legs; or more precisely, "jointed foot")

Class: Insecta (insects)

Order: Odonata (dragonflies and damselflies)

Family: Libellulidae

Genus: *Trithemis*

Species: *Trithemis pallidinervis* (long-legged marsh glider)

Long-legged marsh glider, *Trithemis pallidinervis*

FOREWING

COMPOUND EYES

ANTENNAE

THORAX

HEAD

SIX JOINTED LEGS

Insects breathe through pores in their bodies called spiracles. (See the white circles on the caterpillar above.) The spiracles lead to tubes inside the body (called tracheae). Insects don't have lungs, but like other animals, they breathe by taking in oxygen and letting out carbon dioxide. In some cases, their muscles expand and contract to control the intake of air.

INSECTS' CLOSEST RELATIVES

Insects are members of a larger group of animals we call arthropods. Their closest relatives are members of this group. Besides insects, other arthropods include arachnids (spiders, mites, and scorpions), crustaceans (crabs, lobsters, shrimp, and barnacles), myriapods (millipedes and centipedes), sea spiders, and horseshoe crabs. Of all the arthropods on earth, insects make up the vast majority of species.

Arthropods have jointed legs. They also have a segmented body and a hard external skeleton, or exoskeleton. The inside of an arthropod is a cavity full of fluids. These internal fluids are similar to our blood.

Red crab from Mandarmani, India. Its head and thorax are fused together and covered by a hard shell called a carapace. The crab's eyes are on stalks that help it see in all directions.

Argiope spider in its web. Spiders—along with scorpions, ticks, and mites— differ from insects in the number of body parts and legs they have.

Horseshoe crabs from Thailand. These arthropods are not true crabs but are related to extinct sea scorpions. The hinged shell covers the crab's body, including its legs.

This scorpion has powerful claws for grasping and a venomous stinger on the tip of its long, segmented abdomen.

15

FOSSIL BUGS

Throughout their history, when insects died, some of them left behind impressions or imprints of themselves, which became fossilized.

According to these fossil records, the first winged insects were the mayflies, grasshoppers, and cockroaches. They appeared about 350 million years ago. That's about 120 million years before the appearance of the earliest dinosaurs!

Then, over a period of time that began 145 million years ago, the first flowering plants appeared. As flowering plants evolved, an explosion of diverse forms of insects followed—many of which were pollinators (like bees) and plant-eaters (like butterfly and moth larvae).

Ancient insects became fossilized if they met certain conditions. Some fell into sticky tree resin that over the years turned into a transparent, golden, stone-like substance called amber. Insects that fossilized in amber reveal lots of detail. Other insects were buried in materials like clay and sand that over millions of years turned into sedimentary rock. Inside the rock, the insect's flattened body made an imprint (or impression). Certain fossils can reveal more than just an impression. They can also hold the blackened (carbonized) remains of the insect. Other fossils are mineralized replacements of the original insect, meaning that the space that once held the insect's body was filled in over time with minerals.

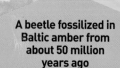

A beetle fossilized in Baltic amber from about 50 million years ago

Where Insects Go in Winter

Depending on the species, they may migrate to warmer locations, find shelter from the cold, or hibernate until warmer weather. Many insects have a type of antifreeze in their body that keeps ice crystals from forming. They may hibernate at any point in their life cycle.

A well-preserved prehistoric grasshopper in amber. Size of insect: 0.5 inch (13 mm).

This is the oldest known full-bodied fossil of an ancient insect, which resembles a dragonfly. It is estimated to be 312 million years old and was found in Massachusetts. When the insect was alive, it left its imprint in mud.

INSECT DIVERSITY

About one million species of insects have been described and named. Sometimes it takes years after discovery to describe and name a new species. It's hard to say exactly how many insects there are worldwide because new species are being described all the time, so the number is always increasing. But that's not all. There are many more species that have yet to be discovered.

Scientists have only been able to come up with rough estimates of the total number of insect species in the world. And those estimates range from 3 to 100 million species, with many agreeing on an estimate of at least 30 million. This means there are plenty of new insects for future generations of scientists—like you—to discover and study!

Insects and other invertebrates make up an impressive 95 percent of all animal species. And vertebrates, the animals people are most familiar with (including mammals, birds, reptiles, amphibians, and fish), make up only about 5 percent of all animals.

Insect diversity is highest in the tropical areas of the world, especially in the treetops of the rain forest. In tropical rain forests, a large portion of the insects are beetles. In the coldest climates, insect diversity is the lowest. Some insect groups found in the coldest climates include icebugs, dagger flies, and balloon flies.

Some insects are found over a large area that covers different continents, while others have smaller distributions. Often, non-migratory insects that live in isolated places like on islands and mountaintops are not found anywhere else.

This snail is but one of many invertebrates.

Mammals, like this tiger, make up less than one percent of all animals.

DIVERSITY OF THE ANIMAL KINGDOM

INVERTEBRATES 95.6%

MAMMALS 0.4%

AMPHIBIANS 0.5%

REPTILES 0.6%

BIRDS 0.7%

FISH 2.2%

PERCENTAGE OF INVERTEBRATES BY GROUP

INSECTS 71.1%

MOLLUSKS 8.5%

CRUSTACEANS 4.3%

SPIDERS 3.1%

OTHER INVERTEBRATES 13.0%

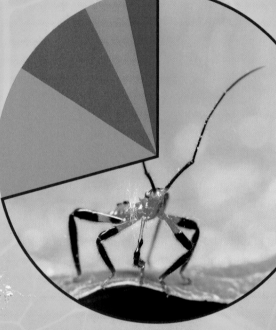

PERCENTAGE OF INSECTS BY ORDER

BEETLES 40.0%

TRUE BUGS 8.2%

SMALLER INSECT ORDERS 9.4%

FLIES 12.0%

ANTS, BEES, WASPS, SAWFLIES 13.0%

BUTTERFLIES & MOTHS 17.4%

LIFE CYCLE OF AN INSECT

After hatching from its egg, a young insect grows until its skin, or exoskeleton, gets too tight. Then, it must shed its old skin, or molt. As it grows, an insect goes through a series of stages between molts.

Insects also go through some developmental changes as they mature. These changes are referred to as metamorphosis. There are two kinds of metamorphosis: simple and complete.

In species such as grasshoppers and true bugs, which undergo **simple metamorphosis,** there are three stages: the egg, nymph, and adult. The immature insect is called a nymph. Nymphs generally look like miniature versions of the adult, minus the wings. In species that develop wings, the nymphs have little wing buds visible on their backs.

In species such as butterflies and beetles, which go through **complete metamorphosis,** there are four stages: the egg, larva, pupa, and adult. The juvenile insect is called a larva. The larva looks very different from the adult insect. In order to transform into an adult, it must first go through an inactive stage, when it is called a pupa. During this stage, the larval tissues break down and adult tissues form—including the wings. When the time is right, a newly formed adult breaks out of the pupal skin and expands its wings. For protection, some insect larvae spin a silk cocoon before transforming into a pupa. The cocoon is a protective covering, like a blanket.

Life Cycle of a Grasshopper: Simple Metamorphosis

The two-striped grasshopper (*Melanoplus bivittatus*) typically lays its eggs in soil, where they will stay over winter. In the spring, when they hatch, tiny nymphs emerge and begin eating plants. As the nymphs grow, they molt a few times. At each stage of their development, their future wings grow. When the nymph molts for the last time, the emerging adult has fully developed wings and can fly.

Life Cycle of a Monarch Butterfly: Complete Metamorphosis

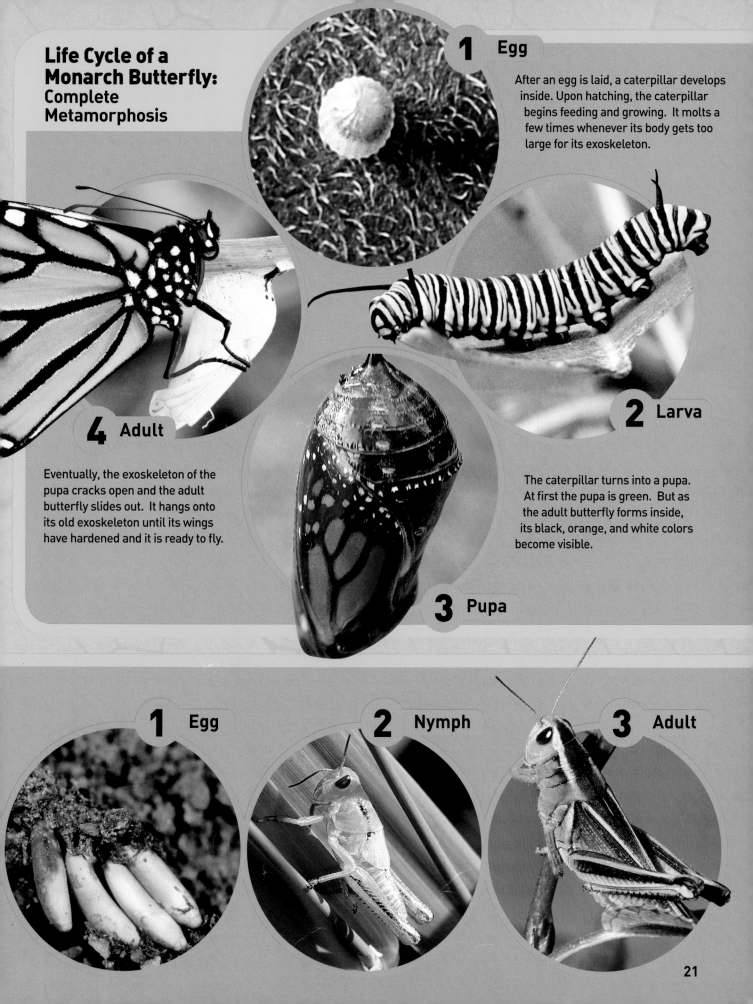

1 Egg

After an egg is laid, a caterpillar develops inside. Upon hatching, the caterpillar begins feeding and growing. It molts a few times whenever its body gets too large for its exoskeleton.

2 Larva

The caterpillar turns into a pupa. At first the pupa is green. But as the adult butterfly forms inside, its black, orange, and white colors become visible.

3 Pupa

4 Adult

Eventually, the exoskeleton of the pupa cracks open and the adult butterfly slides out. It hangs onto its old exoskeleton until its wings have hardened and it is ready to fly.

1 Egg

2 Nymph

3 Adult

COURTSHIP, MATING, AND EGG-LAYING

Finding a suitable mate is a challenge for insects. In addition to visual cues like color patterns, airborne chemicals called pheromones help insects locate possible mates. Courtship can involve dancing, gift giving, serenading, touching, and blinking their lights to entice a partner to mate. Many insects also use sound or surface vibrations.

The mating process involves contact between a male and female in order to fertilize the eggs. Hoverflies, butterflies, and other winged insects sometimes even mate in flight.

After laying eggs, most insects don't hang around to care for their young. That doesn't mean they don't try to improve their offsprings' chances of survival, though. Insects may prepare nests in advance or carefully select just the right host plant for laying their eggs.

Species in which one or both of the parents care for their young include social insects like ants, wasps, and termites. (See "Social Insects" on pp. 40–41.)

The male dance fly courts the female by offering her a nuptial gift. She eats the gift while mating.

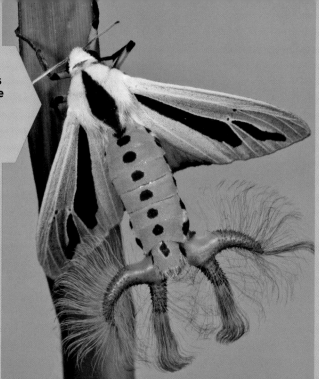

To find a mate, a male *Creatonotos gangis* moth turns its greenish scent organ inside out from the end of its abdomen. It secretes a pheromone that attracts females of its species.

After courtship, a pair of tiny hairstreak butterflies mate on a leaf, after which the female will seek host plants to lay her fertilized eggs.

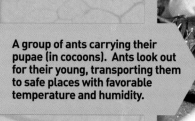

A group of ants carrying their pupae (in cocoons). Ants look out for their young, transporting them to safe places with favorable temperature and humidity.

INSECT EGGS AND EGG CASES

Female insects tend to lay many eggs—up to thousands over their lifetime. By laying so many eggs, they improve the chances that a few of their young will survive. Insect eggs come in many different shapes, colors, and sizes, depending on the species. The eggs might be bundled in silk cases, or set in jelly-like (gelatinous) masses. Some eggs have long stalks, and some are glued to tree branches. The females of most types of insects lay eggs, but aphids, some moths and flies, and a few cockroach species give birth to live young, meaning the eggs hatch before the babies are born.

A leopard lacewing butterfly laying her eggs on a vine tendril

A large cluster of eggs of the cabbage butterfly

A stink bug in the process of laying her eggs

Many young mantises stream out of the bottom of a large egg case made by their mother.

Some lacewings lay their eggs on the end of a stalk, which may then attach to a plant, wood, or even a windowsill.

PUPAE

The pupa is the resting stage between larva and adult in insects that undergo complete metamorphosis. Pupae may appear quiet on the outside, but on the inside, their larval body is breaking down and their new body as a winged adult is forming. The seemingly helpless pupae have some special ways of protecting themselves. A few are able to wriggle if touched or even walk around. Some pupae can make sounds or vibrate to scare predators. Some secrete toxic chemicals to avoid being eaten. Others, especially certain butterfly pupae, are defended by ants. (See the alcon blue butterfly, p. 222.) The pupae of bees, wasps, and ants remain in their hives or nests and are protected by adults of their species. Other insects spend their time as pupae underground, on trees and branches, or underwater.

Two black swallowtail caterpillars transforming into pupae. The one above is almost finished shedding its larval skin. Both are supported by silk strands connecting them to the branch.

A tomato hornworm caterpillar under attack by parasitoid wasps. After feeding on the caterpillar, the wasp larvae spin white silk cocoons and turn into pupae inside it.

A monarch butterfly emerges from its pupal exoskeleton. Once out, the butterfly will hang from the exoskeleton as its wings expand.

Two adult worker ants carrying an ant pupa

A mosquito pupa floating near the surface of the water. It leaves the water as an adult.

BUG SENSES

Bugs have the same senses of sight, taste, smell, hearing, and touch that we do, but they work in a very different way from our own senses. Imagine if we could taste with our feet and hear with ears on our legs, or see in front of and behind us at the same time.

TASTE

Insects taste mainly with their mouthparts and their feet. Some insects, such as bees, also have taste receptors on their antennae. And female wasps and crickets can determine by taste where to lay their eggs, using the egg-laying organ (ovipositor) on the end of their abdomen.

COMPOUND EYES

SIMPLE EYES

Gulf Fritillary butterfly

Fly

SIGHT

Insects see with simple or compound eyes—many have both types, and a few have no eyes at all. Simple eyes can't focus on images, but merely distinguish between light and dark. Many larvae and termites have simple eyes. Compound eyes, with their faceted lenses, can see objects in color and detail. Insects with large compound eyes can see in all directions. A honeybee's compound eyes are able to see a wider range of colors than most insects because they have three color pigment receptors, like us, rather than the two that most insects have.

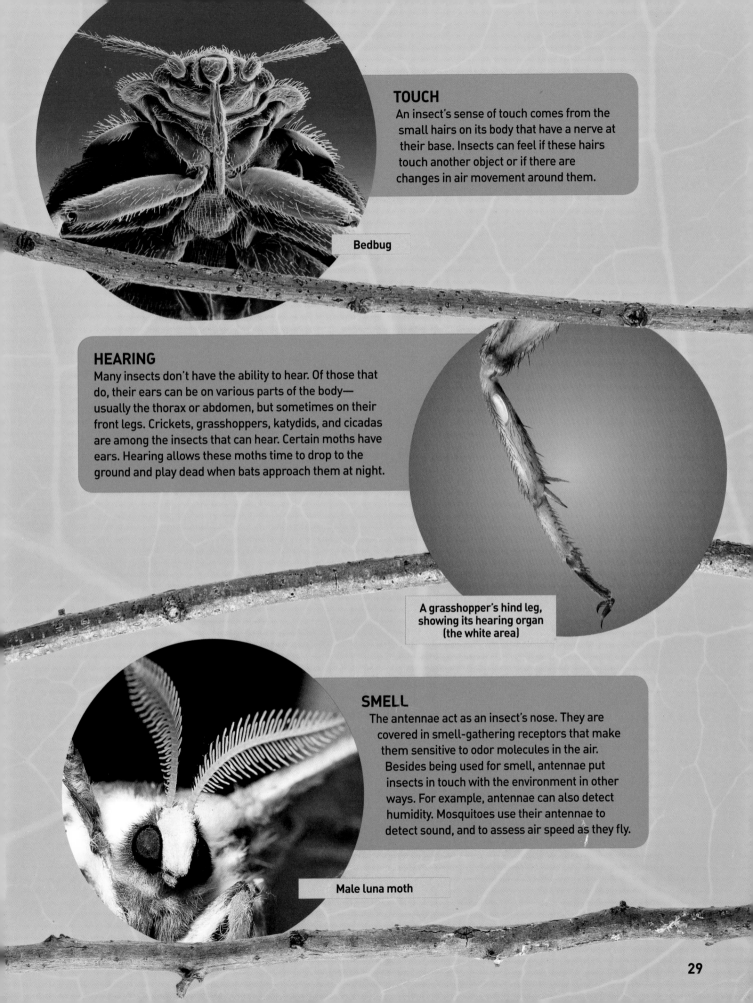

TOUCH

An insect's sense of touch comes from the small hairs on its body that have a nerve at their base. Insects can feel if these hairs touch another object or if there are changes in air movement around them.

Bedbug

HEARING

Many insects don't have the ability to hear. Of those that do, their ears can be on various parts of the body—usually the thorax or abdomen, but sometimes on their front legs. Crickets, grasshoppers, katydids, and cicadas are among the insects that can hear. Certain moths have ears. Hearing allows these moths time to drop to the ground and play dead when bats approach them at night.

A grasshopper's hind leg, showing its hearing organ (the white area)

SMELL

The antennae act as an insect's nose. They are covered in smell-gathering receptors that make them sensitive to odor molecules in the air. Besides being used for smell, antennae put insects in touch with the environment in other ways. For example, antennae can also detect humidity. Mosquitoes use their antennae to detect sound, and to assess air speed as they fly.

Male luna moth

ANTENNAE

Insect antennae come in many forms.

The antennae are made up of a row of segments. Each segment is jointed, so the antennae bend, and each segment can have its own shape. The segments can be simple and straight—like those of mayflies, cockroaches, and caddisflies. The antennae can be clubbed on the ends, as in butterflies. They can be rounded or plate-like, as in many beetles. And they can be feathery, like those of many moths and flies. In ants and weevils, the antennae are bent in the middle.

The male cecropia moth has large feathery antennae. It is in the same silk moth family as the luna moth on p. 29. Females have thinner antennae than males.

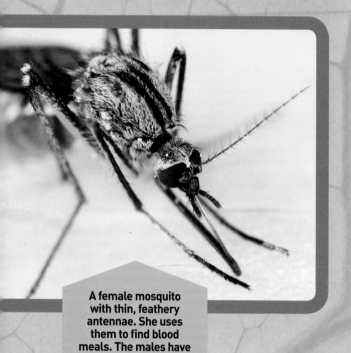

A female mosquito with thin, feathery antennae. She uses them to find blood meals. The males have bushier antennae for finding females.

A Red Admiral butterfly. Butterfly antennae are knobbed on the tips. They can detect the smells of nectar and pheromones.

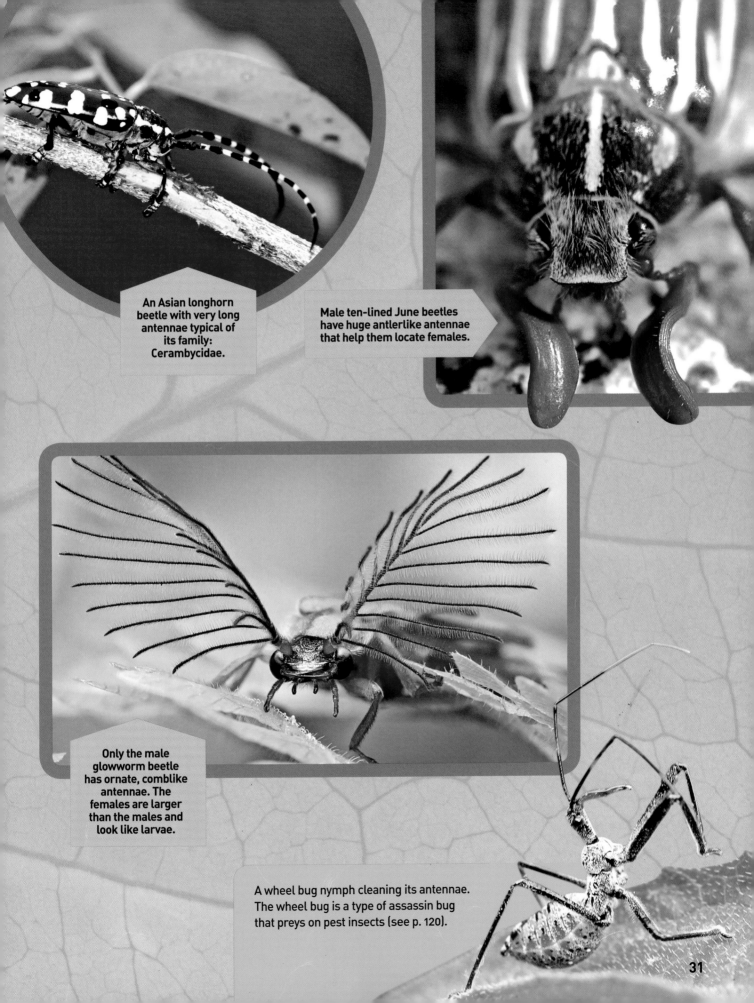

An Asian longhorn beetle with very long antennae typical of its family: Cerambycidae.

Male ten-lined June beetles have huge antlerlike antennae that help them locate females.

Only the male glowworm beetle has ornate, comblike antennae. The females are larger than the males and look like larvae.

A wheel bug nymph cleaning its antennae. The wheel bug is a type of assassin bug that preys on pest insects (see p. 120).

HOW BUGS "TALK"

People communicate both verbally and nonverbally with other people. We talk, make noises, make faces, gesture, touch, and use scents. Insects do similar things. They communicate with sounds, visual signals, touching, and also by using their sense of smell. They communicate in order to find mates, escape predators, mimic other insects, warn of danger, threaten others, and give directions to food sources or other resources.

Insects make sounds by rubbing their body parts together (called stridulating), and by hissing, tapping, and vibrating their wings or special sound-producing membranes. They communicate visually with color patterns, body movement, and light flashes. Several types of insects, such as fireflies and glowworms, have light-emitting organs that glow in the dark.

Touching is an especially important form of communication for insects that can't hear and don't see well. For example, when ants and termites run in a line, they use their antennae to tap the hind legs of the individual in front of them, as if to say "I'm still behind you."

Insects communicate by smell using chemical odors called pheromones. They emit these odors, or messages, into the air. In addition to the pheromones that attract mates, insects use other odors in making food trails and for sounding the alarm to members of their species when danger is near.

A male African monarch communicates his interest to a potential mate. The male has two brushlike organs that it pushes out at the end of its abdomen. The "brushes" disperse pheromones in the air.

Fireflies "talk" to each other with light signals (above). The pattern of blinking can signal different things, such as an interest in finding a mate or in defending a territory.

Ants communicate with each other through visual signals, sounds, touch, and pheromones. The two ants at left, with their powerful jaws, are threatening to attack each other.

FOOD AND FEEDING

Many insects—especially those with complete metamorphosis—change what they eat when they grow up. For example, the caterpillars of butterflies and moths typically chew leaves, but as adults they drink nectar or other liquids.

An insect's mouthparts correspond with its diet. For instance, the proboscis of a butterfly or moth is long and hollow for reaching into flowers to drink nectar. The proboscis coils up when the meal is over. The group of insects called true bugs have a combined proboscis and hardened beak to pierce plants and drink their sap. Both mosquitoes and aphids can pierce and suck—the mosquito to feed on animal blood and the aphid to feed on plant fluids. Insects that chew their food feed with a pair of mandibles that can cut, tear, and crush. Meat-eating insects tend to have knife-like mandibles, whereas plant-eating insects have flatter, wider ones. Some mandibles are modified for fighting and hunting.

Host plants are the source of food for many larval and adult insects. Some insects can survive on only one species of host plant. For this reason, these species are called specialists. Other insects can eat various plants and are considered generalists. The larvae of a few generalists, like the gypsy moth, will eat just about any kind of leaf. Large groups of them can remove the leaves from a patch of forest.

A praying mantis holds a grasshopper with a vice-like grip while feeding on it.

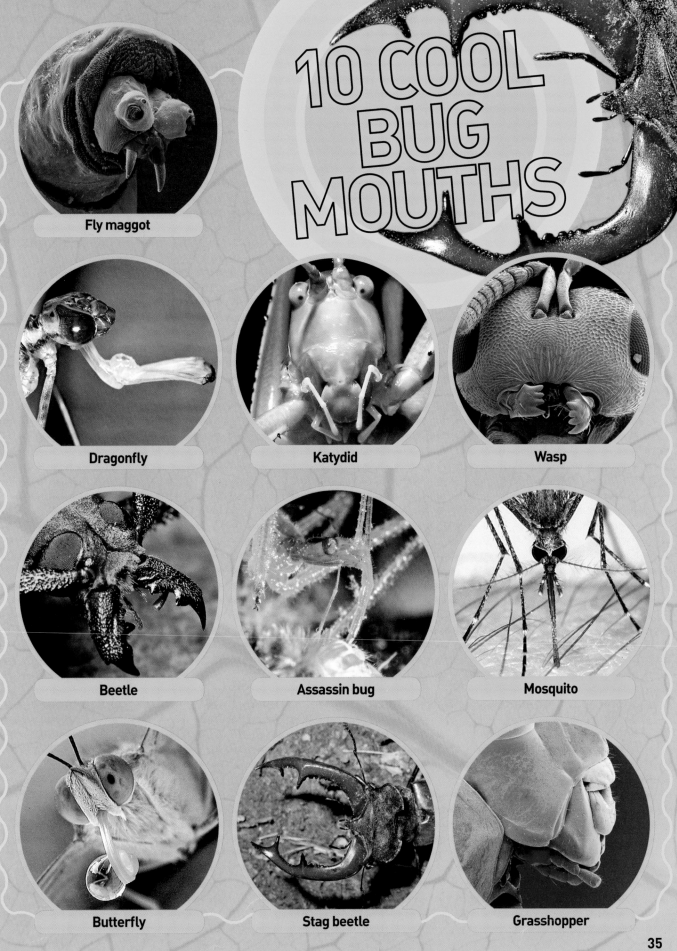

10 COOL BUG MOUTHS

Fly maggot

Dragonfly

Katydid

Wasp

Beetle

Assassin bug

Mosquito

Butterfly

Stag beetle

Grasshopper

WHERE BUGS LIVE

Insects are found just about anywhere on Earth—from the polar regions to rain forests, from treetops to underground, as well as underwater, in houses, on animals, and on and inside of plants. One group of insects called sea skaters is even found on the surface of the ocean. Over time, insects have adapted to every available habitat where they can find resources. Special adaptations allow them to survive in places with extreme conditions, such as the freezing-cold Arctic, and the dry Namib desert, which gets only a half inch (13 mm) of rain per year. With the exception of the water striders, there are no insects in the open ocean.

Many insects require more than one habitat over their life spans. For example, some insects may live underground or underwater as larvae or nymphs, and aboveground as adults.

Mosquitoes are found in moist environments and their larvae live in standing water. Adult females need occasional blood meals.

These termites march with nest-mates in search of new sources of dead wood in the forest.

Caterpillars can often be found on the undersurface of leaves, where they're less visible to passing birds.

Whirligig beetles twirl around on the surface of flowing streams. They can swim, dive, and fly.

Flies are attracted to warm and moist places like animal dung (feces), where they lay their eggs.

Leaf miners are the larvae of several types of insects that feed on an inner layer of leaf tissue, making visible trails as they move along.

Two spotted cucumber beetles on a flower. They sometimes feed on pollen when they're not eating the green parts of plants.

Wasps often build their nests in protective locations, like under the eaves of houses.

INSECTS IN NATURE

Insects form an important link in the food chain. They provide food for birds, lizards, mammals, fish, amphibians, spiders, and other insects. If insects were to disappear off the face of the earth, there would be a chain reaction, and many other animals and plants that depend on them would become extinct. We rely on insects to pollinate crops, make honey, make silk, and clean up the environment. Scientists use insects like *Drosophila* flies (fruit flies) for research. Gardeners use predatory insects to get rid of plant-eating pests. And in some parts of the world, people eat protein-rich insects as part of their diet.

Small as they are, insects play major roles in the environment, and whether they are herbivores, predators, parasites, or parasitoids determines what part they play. They are herbivores if they feed on plants; predators if they kill small animals for food; parasites if they get their nutrients from living on or inside another animal without killing it; and parasitoids if they live as parasites but eventually kill their host.

Insects may engage in a "mutualistic" partnership with other organisms such as plants. This means that both the plant and the insect benefit from each other. A classic example of mutualism is pollination. The plant gets fertilized, and the insect typically gets rewarded with nectar, pollen, or resin. About 85 percent of flowering plants depend on insects for pollination—and that includes many of our crop plants such as apples and broccoli.

Some insects have a special role in cleaning up the environment. They may chew up the wood of fallen trees, recycle animal dung, and even break down dead animal bodies. They perform tasks that people don't want to do, and by burrowing and burying, they do wonders to improve the soil.

A brown anole lizard with a cicada in its mouth. The lizard's entire diet consists of insects.

After attacking a honeybee, these African driver ants are carrying it back to their nest, along a clothesline.

A bumblebee drinks nectar and gets covered in pollen.

Parasites feed on many insects. Some are fairly harmless like the tiny mites covering this beetle.

These tiny caterpillars are eating a willow leaf. Once the leaf is eaten, the group will move on to other leaves. The larvae of many insects have entirely different diets from the adults of their species.

SOCIAL INSECTS

Some insects are solitary and others naturally group together, like a cluster of ladybugs or certain caterpillars, when they feed in a row on the edge of a leaf. But truly social (or eusocial) insects have a system with special tasks for each member. Social insects include all ants, all termites, and many bees and wasps.

Social insects have certain features in common. They live together in a nest. They tend their young. They have overlapping generations—meaning that new insects are constantly being produced in a colony—and they have a division of labor, or caste system, in which members carry out specific tasks. Their castes include "reproductives," which are the queens and drones. The task of queens and drones, besides reproducing, is to select a location for a colony and to begin preparing the new nest. Other caste members, including workers and soldiers, don't reproduce. Workers are responsible for cleaning the nest; caring for eggs, larvae, pupae, and the queen; and collecting food. Soldiers defend the colony from predators.

Workers of a paper wasp colony build the hive and tend the young. If the queen wasp happens to die, one of the workers will replace her.

Look at the difference in shape and relative size of these three leafcutter ants. They belong to the same species—*Atta cephalotes*. The largest is a queen, whose sole responsibility is to reproduce, and the other two are workers: a major and a minor.

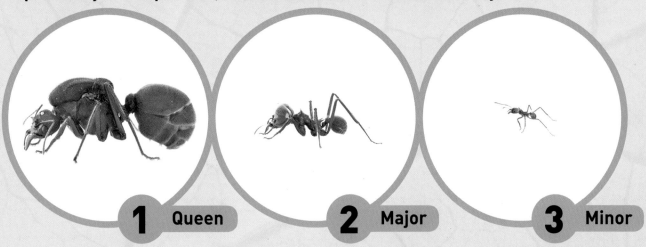

1 Queen   **2** Major   **3** Minor

The nymphs of true bugs often group together as a large family. They are social in one sense, but not eusocial like insects with a caste system.

Worker ants from one colony of weaver ants are working together to bridge a gap between two leaves. Once the bridge is established, other ants can cross over it.

COLORS AND PATTERNS

The incredible colors and designs on insects like beetles and butterflies help them to recognize each other, to impress mates, and to avoid predators. The colors and patterns are mostly determined by an insect's genes.

There are two types of colors in insects. One comes from pigments (or dyes) that are in their exoskeleton or below its surface. For example, bloodworms (the larvae of a type of insect called a midge) are red because of the color of their body fluids. The other type of color is formed optically, by the reflection of light off the surface of the insect's body. The three-dimensional texture is responsible for the colors we see. Optical colors can look metallic or iridescent— shifting as you see them from different angles.

The scales covering the wings and bodies of butterflies and moths can have either type of color and often have both. The striking, iridescent wings of blue Morpho butterflies and Madagascan sunset moths are examples of optical colors. Flies, dragonflies, and other clear-winged insects have optical color patterns that they display by holding their wings at certain angles.

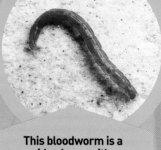

This bloodworm is a midge larva with a transparent exoskeleton. Hemoglobin, found mostly in vertebrates, is a red protein that gives the larva its bright red color.

The Madagascan sunset moth has iridescent green on the forewings and various iridescent colors on the hind wings.

A solitary black bumblebee from India with iridescent wings

Close-up of iridescent blue scales from a butterfly's wing. The fine texture on each scale produces the color we see.

An iridescent green damselfly with transparent, blue-green wings

DEFENSES

Being near the bottom of the food chain, insects are surrounded by predators—
mammals, birds, reptiles, amphibians, fish, and various arthropods. As a result, they have evolved an incredible array of defenses in order to survive. Take chemical defenses, for one. Many insects have poisonous or bad-tasting chemicals in their bodies. Some, like bees and wasps, can sting. Others spit or shoot acid at their foes, or they release foul-smelling chemicals.

Mimicry is also a widespread defense. Butterflies often mimic each other's color patterns for protection. There are insects that look like spiders, and spiders that look like insects. Some insects have false faces with real-looking eyes (see pp. 46–47). And there are insects that use camouflage to hide in plain sight by resembling leaves, sticks, or other things in their environment. Additional adaptations that protect insects include spines, horns, sharp mandibles, and a thick exoskeleton.

Running, jumping, wriggling, flying away, and hiding are other ways insects avoid being eaten. If insects can't find hideouts, some will make their own by rolling leaves or creating other forms of shelter. Some insects confront their enemies by fighting them. In a pinch, others even shed appendages—the monkey slug caterpillar, for example, sheds its false legs—in order to escape.

Most impressive is how many insects use a variety of defenses. If one doesn't work, perhaps another will!

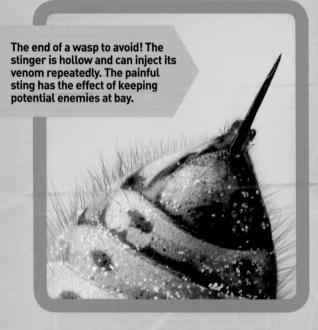

The end of a wasp to avoid! The stinger is hollow and can inject its venom repeatedly. The painful sting has the effect of keeping potential enemies at bay.

A bombardier beetle sprays a boiling-hot chemical when it feels threatened. It has excellent aim, and it can cause intense pain.

A female clouded sulphur butterfly blends in with the leaves that surround it. Many insects rely on camouflage to be invisible to predators.

This saddleback caterpillar stings anything that comes too close to its hollow, venom-filled spines.

A green katydid resembles a leaf in color and pattern.

FALSE FACES

Birds are major predators of insects.

But while hunting they can be spooked by anything resembling snakes or other bird-eating predators. If they don't react quickly, they might be eaten themselves! Insects have evolved ways to take advantage of this fear in birds and other animals that hunt using their sense of sight. Some insects have false faces with fake eyes, and some have eyespots that create the appearance of a spooky face staring back at you. Birds are easily startled by such false faces or eyes, giving the insect another chance to survive. Some false faces, however, may not be adaptations, but chance patterns that we mistakenly interpret as faces.

A polyphemus moth in a defensive posture, its hind wings exposing a pair of fake eyes

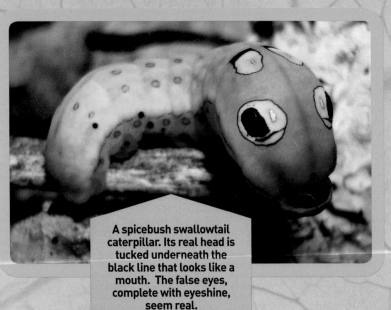

A spicebush swallowtail caterpillar. Its real head is tucked underneath the black line that looks like a mouth. The false eyes, complete with eyeshine, seem real.

The pupa (or chrysalis) of the darius butterfly mimics a viper. It has a wide, false snake-shaped head with false snake-like eyes.

The comical face on the back of this shield bug may not be a real adaptation to frighten predators, but its coloration may warn that it's toxic.

The io moth normally has its hind wings covered while it rests. If a bird approaches, it lifts its forewings to expose giant fake eyes.

The Oleander hawkmoth caterpillar has a pair of false eyes in a fold on its back. When disturbed (right), it tucks its head down and flashes its huge false eyes. When at rest (below), its false eyes are half closed.

THE SILK MAKERS

Spiders spin silk threads for webs. But did you know that at some point in their lives, many insects make silk threads too? The silk is a liquid inside the silk glands of insects and spiders, but when it is secreted from the glands and exposed to air, it dries into silk strands. Both insects and spiders use silk threads for many purposes, such as for making cocoons, traps, safe havens, drag lines, coverings for their eggs, and support structures, as well as for molting, wrapping prey, and ballooning (using the wind to blow them to another location).

Silk is a natural fiber composed of proteins. It is exceptionally strong and elastic. The larvae of most butterflies and moths and various other insects secrete silk from spinnerets below the mouth. But, insects called webspinners secrete silk from glands in their front legs. They work together to make their homes of silken tunnels and sheets on tree trunks, rocks, and leaf litter.

These ties are made from the unwound cocoons of the silk moth. The silk threads are dyed and woven into fabric.

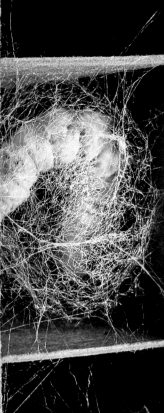

Two silkworm caterpillars making their cocoons

10 COOL INSECT SILK MAKERS

Moth larvae

Webspinner nymphs

Some wasp and bee larvae

Raspy crickets

Fungus gnat larvae

Weaver ant larvae

Caddisfly larvae

Lacewings (egg stalks)

Black fly larvae

Butterfly larvae

MIGRATION

A number of animals—many birds, some whales, African elephants, caribou— migrate, and so do insects. Insects that migrate include Australia's Bogong moths, and many species of dragonflies, beetles, and butterflies, such as the well-known monarch. As with other animals, reasons that insects migrate include escaping drought or cold and finding food.

One of life's big mysteries has been exactly how animals migrate. When monarchs migrate, they use the sun as a compass. But the sun changes position in the sky over the day. Despite this, monarchs are able to keep flying in a particular direction. Scientists have been trying to learn how this happens. They have discovered a molecular process in the butterfly's antennae that compensates for the sun's shifting position.

Scientists also think that monarchs might use a magnetic compass that informs them where to go. Monarchs have a mineral in their bodies called magnetite. This mineral is the most magnetic on earth. It's found not just in monarchs, but also in some other insects such as bees, dragonflies, termites, and grasshoppers, as well as in migrating birds. It appears to play a role in insect migration, and scientists are actively researching this possibility.

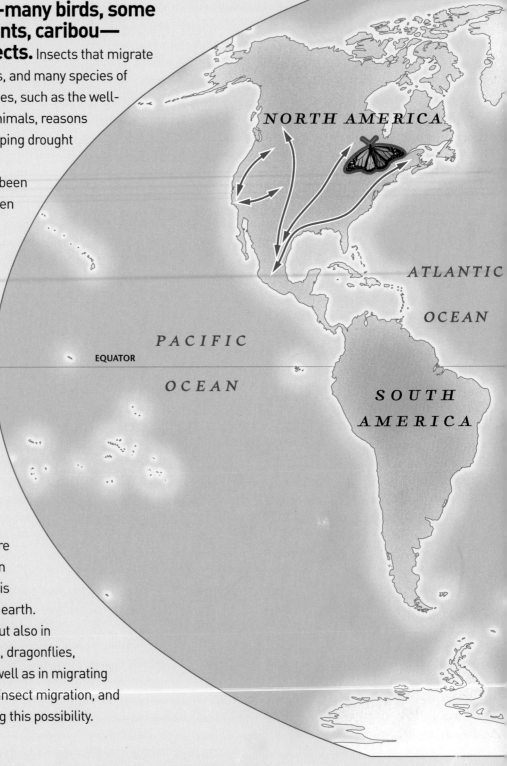

NORTH AMERICA

ATLANTIC

OCEAN

PACIFIC

EQUATOR

OCEAN

SOUTH
AMERICA

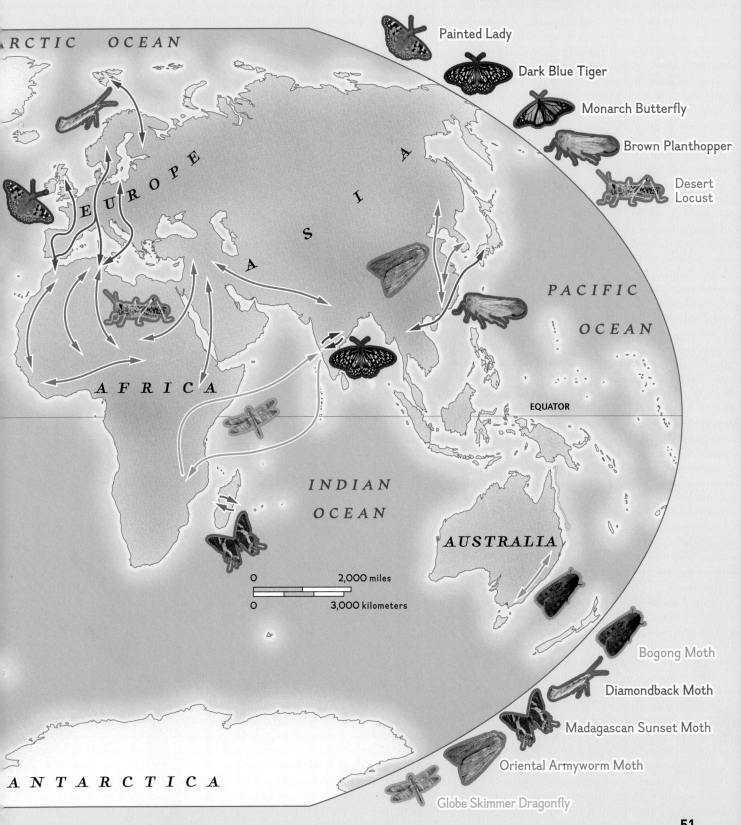

Migration routes shown are some of the longer examples for the particular species.

ARCTIC OCEAN

EUROPE

ASIA

AFRICA

PACIFIC OCEAN

EQUATOR

INDIAN OCEAN

AUSTRALIA

ANTARCTICA

Painted Lady

Dark Blue Tiger

Monarch Butterfly

Brown Planthopper

Desert Locust

Bogong Moth

Diamondback Moth

Madagascan Sunset Moth

Oriental Armyworm Moth

Globe Skimmer Dragonfly

0   2,000 miles

0   3,000 kilometers

INSECTS AS PESTS

Less than one percent of insects are considered serious pests, yet their effect is impossible to ignore. Insect pests damage crops, eat wooden structures, sting, bite, ruin lawns and gardens, and make loud noises.

Lice, bedbugs, fleas, some flies, and some mosquitoes are pests—taking blood meals and leaving irritating rashes and bites. And some mosquitoes can endanger human health by carrying diseases like malaria. Malaria is a serious parasitic disease that affects about 300 million people around the world. About one million people die from it each year.

Ticks, related to spiders, also bite and can transmit microorganisms that cause human disease (such as Lyme disease and Rocky Mountain spotted fever). Chiggers, also related to spiders, can transmit illness, and they cause serious itching and leave red welts.

Locusts are grasshoppers that form huge swarms. "Plagues" of locusts can darken the sky as they fly into an area, and then eat everything in sight before moving on. The desert locust has such a reputation in drier parts of Africa.

Pest management has become a huge industry in which professional entomologists try to control the numbers of certain insect species. One means of controlling insect pests without pesticides is through biological pest control. Living organisms like predators and parasites are employed to do the job. Entomologists also help to protect species that are not pests.

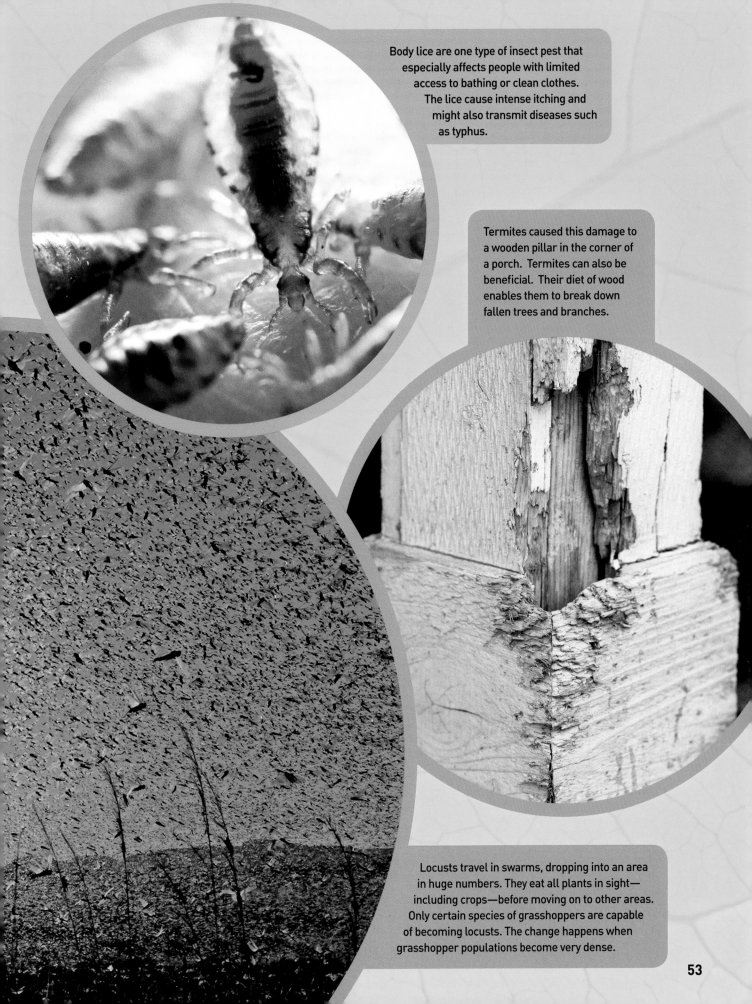

Body lice are one type of insect pest that especially affects people with limited access to bathing or clean clothes. The lice cause intense itching and might also transmit diseases such as typhus.

Termites caused this damage to a wooden pillar in the corner of a porch. Termites can also be beneficial. Their diet of wood enables them to break down fallen trees and branches.

Locusts travel in swarms, dropping into an area in huge numbers. They eat all plants in sight—including crops—before moving on to other areas. Only certain species of grasshoppers are capable of becoming locusts. The change happens when grasshopper populations become very dense.

THE THREAT OF INSECT EXTINCTION

As human populations expand, people use more and more natural resources, and in the process, they alter the natural environment. Most of the earth's land surface, about 83 percent, has been altered by humans. As a consequence of our activities, certain animals, including insects, have become extinct— which means they will never be seen again. And many other animals are in danger of extinction right now. Scientists estimate that many insects are disappearing even before they are discovered and named!

The aim of conservation is to preserve and protect animals and plants, their natural environments, and the ecosystems they live in. And where natural areas have been damaged, people are making efforts to restore them to their previously healthy condition.

When we help animals, plants, and the environment, we help ourselves too!

As Harvard biologist E. O. Wilson once wrote, "So important are insects and other land-dwelling arthropods, that if all were to disappear, humanity probably could not last more than a few months."

The erosion and loss of insects' natural habitats alters the balance of nature. One problem facing us is how to manage land in order to maintain biodiversity and a healthy ecosystem.

10 CHALLENGES INSECTS FACE

Water pollution

Deforestation

Air pollution

Industrial waste (in water)

Climate change (flooding)

Building construction

Industrial waste (on land)

Climate change (drought)

Habitat degradation

Overuse of pesticides

SIMPLE
METAMORPHOSIS

A newly emerged skimmer dragonfly hanging from its nymphal exoskeleton

Balloon-winged katydid nymph from Australia

A katydid nymph perched on a flower bud

Blue darner dragonfly

A Chinese mantis nymph
on a child's finger

An assassin bug sliding out
of its old exoskeleton

INSECT ORDERS

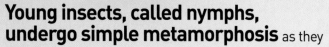

Young insects, called nymphs, undergo simple metamorphosis as they grow up, which means they often look like miniature versions of the adult insects they will become. Many, but not all, insects with this form of metamorphosis will develop wings. The ones that do have wing buds visible on their backs while they're nymphs.

Insects are in the kingdom Animalia, the phylum Arthropoda, and the class Insecta. On these two pages, you'll find all the different orders of insects with simple metamorphosis. The scientific name for the order is noted below the common name and is followed by its pronunciation. The figures below it are estimates of the number of species in that order that have already been named and described. To find out about some of the different insects within an order, just turn to the pages noted.

TRUE BUGS
Hemiptera
hem · IP · tur · uh
About 82,000 species
pp. 100–131

GRASSHOPPERS, KATYDIDS, AND CRICKETS
Orthoptera
or · THOP · tur · uh
About 22,000 species
pp. 80–89

TERMITES AND COCKROACHES
Blattodea
blat · toe · dee · uh
About 6,600 species
pp. 94–95

There are three orders with insects that undergo simple metamorphosis that aren't included in the profiles that start on page 60. They are:

BOOKLICE AND BARKLICE
Psocoptera
so · COP · ter · uh
About 5,500 species of small, scavenging insects

WEBSPINNERS
Embioptera
em · bee · OP · ter · uh
About 400 described species of insects that spin silk from glands on their legs and live inside silk structures

ANGEL INSECTS
Zoraptera
zor · APP · ter · uh
About 33 species of tiny, termite-like insects that live in rotting wood

DRAGONFLIES AND DAMSELFLIES

Odonata

oh · duh · NA · ta

About 5,680 species

pp. 62–69

THRIPS

Thysanoptera

thigh · san · OP · ter · uh

About 5,000 species

pp. 98–99

STONEFLIES

Plecoptera

pleh · COP · ter · uh

About 3,500 species

pp. 74–75

LICE

Phthiraptera

thur · AP · ter · uh

About 3,000 species

pp. 96–97

An assassin bug nymph

STICK INSECTS AND LEAF INSECTS

Phasmatodea

faz · ma · toe · dee · uh

About 3,000 species

pp. 76–79

MAYFLIES

Ephemeroptera

ih · fem · uh · ROP · ter · uh

About 2,500 species

pp. 60–61

MANTISES

Mantodea

man · TOE · dee · uh

About 2,400 species

pp. 90–93

EARWIGS

Dermaptera

der · MAP · ter · uh

About 2,000 species

pp. 70–71

ICEBUGS AND GLADIATORS

Notoptera (also called *Grylloblattodea*)

no · TOP · ter · uh

About 26 species

pp. 72–73

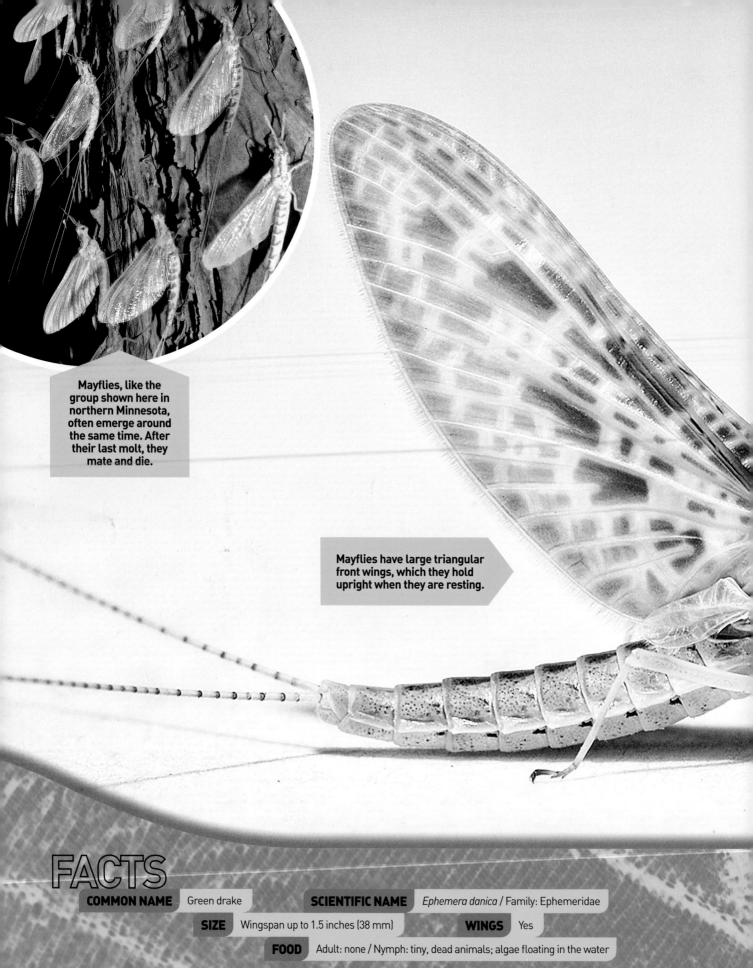

Mayflies, like the group shown here in northern Minnesota, often emerge around the same time. After their last molt, they mate and die.

Mayflies have large triangular front wings, which they hold upright when they are resting.

FACTS

COMMON NAME Green drake

SCIENTIFIC NAME *Ephemera danica* / Family: Ephemeridae

SIZE Wingspan up to 1.5 inches (38 mm)

WINGS Yes

FOOD Adult: none / Nymph: tiny, dead animals; algae floating in the water

GREEN DRAKE MAYFLY

FAMILY EPHEMERIDAE

Mayflies belong to a group of insects that first appeared between 354 and 295 million years ago. That makes them one of the world's oldest insects! In spite of their longevity as a group, mayflies have an incredibly short life span. As adults, many species, like the green drake, live only one day! Although many mayflies live only a short time as adults, they can spend up to two years as nymphs. During this time, they go through several molts, maturing a bit each time. Eventually, they develop wings and soon become adults.

Green drakes spend their brief adult life in search of a mate so that they can reproduce. Males and females join together in large swarms that form over bodies of water such as lakes and rivers. After mating, the female deposits her fertilized eggs on the surface of the water. The mating process takes so much energy that the mayflies die soon afterward.

HABITAT	Lakes and rivers with sandy or gravel bottoms
RANGE	Throughout Europe

In German, the common name for mayflies is *Eintagsfliegen*. The word means "one-day flies."

GIANT DARNER DRAGONFLY

FAMILY AESHNIDAE

Darners include some of the world's largest dragonflies. Among them is the Giant Darner, which grows up to 5 inches (127 mm) long and has a wingspan that's about the length of its body.

Darners are fierce predators—even as nymphs. They'll attack just about anything they can snatch, including organisms much bigger than they are. This includes aquatic insects, worms, fish, and small frogs.

How does a nymph seize a big meal? It relies mainly on its labium, an extendible jaw underneath its head. When the nymph gets close enough to its prey, it shoots its labium forward. Hooks on the labium snare the victim and keep it from escaping. The nymph then retracts its labium, dragging the prey to its mouth. Chomp!

This dragonfly nymph extends its labium from underneath its head to grab its prey. After the nymph is done feeding, it will fold its labium away.

Three hundred million years ago dragonflies were about five times larger than those today. Their wings measured about 28 inches (700 mm) from tip to tip. That is greater than the wingspan of some parrots!

FACTS

COMMON NAME	Giant darner
SCIENTIFIC NAME	*Anax walsinghami* / Family: Aeshnidae
SIZE	Wingspan up to 5 inches (127 mm)
WINGS	Yes
FOOD	Adult: small insects / Nymph: aquatic insects, small tadpoles, and fish

A dragonfly's wings contain many veins. The insect's heart pumps blood into its wings through these veins.

HABITAT Streams, ponds, marshes

RANGE Southwestern United States, western Mexico, Honduras

A few dragonfly species migrate long distances. The globe skimmer *(Plata flavascens)* is believed to have the longest migration of any insect. It travels 11,000 miles (17,700 km) across the Indian Ocean to breed.

Male Kirby's dropwing skimmers are a bright orange-red. By contrast, females are yellow.

FACTS

COMMON NAME	Kirby's dropwing skimmer	**SCIENTIFIC NAME**	*Trithemis kirbyi* / Family: Libellulidae
	SIZE	1.3–1.5 inches (35–38 mm) long	**WINGS** Yes
	FOOD	Adult: small insects / Nymph: aquatic insects and small aquatic animals	

KIRBY'S DROPWING SKIMMER

FAMILY LIBELLULIDAE

Currently, there are eleven known families of dragonflies. The largest family is made up of about 1,000 dragonfly species, including Kirby's dropwing skimmer.

Some dragonflies catch their prey while flying, but skimmers prefer to do most of their hunting from a perch. They hang out on objects such as twigs, leaf stalks, and branches, from which they scan the area for food. When their prey is in close range, they dart out to grab the victim, and then return to their perch to eat.

When the male skimmer isn't hunting, it takes flight. It patrols the area for other male dragonflies, which it considers a threat to its food supply, as well as competition in the mating department.

HABITAT Streams, rivers, and pools in savanna, woodland, or bush

RANGE Africa, southern Europe, Middle East, Indian Ocean islands, southern Asia

DRAGONFLIES GALLERY

Dragonflies have fascinated people for centuries. Their brightly colored bodies have inspired works of art, while their sewing-needle shape has given rise to strange legends. According to one tale, dragonflies would sew up the mouths of people who told lies! But in reality, dragonflies are harmless to people. In fact, they eat insects, such as mosquitoes and midges, which can be pests to humans.

Dragonflies have excellent vision. They have two large compound eyes that are about half the size of their heads. The eyes are sensitive to motion, so when hunting for food, dragonflies can easily follow a quick-flying insect. Other dragonflies will wait for their prey to come to them. Dragonfly nymphs are meat-eaters too, but their diet comes from what they find in their aquatic environment.

These insects are diverse and come in many different shapes, sizes, and colors. Want to know more? Check out the six examples shown on these pages.

A Halloween pennant skimmer perches on a plant.

This migrant hawker, with its bright blue and brown body, can be found in northern Africa and southern and central Europe.

The Indian pied paddy skimmer has striking black wings, but it isn't a strong flyer. These dragonflies rarely stray from their breeding sites—usually paddy fields and streams.

Southern darters forming a mating wheel. The male is the red one.

A dragonfly's two large compound eyes consist of thousands of tiny facets that help it see clearly. Two simple eyes visible below them detect light and dark.

Just because predators can easily spot brightly colored dragonflies doesn't mean that they can catch them. Many dragonflies are speedy and can outfly predatory birds.

FACTS

OTHER COMMON NAMES	Giant damselfly, forest giant
SCIENTIFIC NAME	*Microstigma rotundatum* / Family: Pseudostigmatidae
SIZE	Wingspan up to 7.5 inches (190 mm); length up to 4.0 inches (100 mm)
WINGS	Yes
FOOD	Adult: spiders and spider prey / Naiad: mosquito larvae, flies, tadpoles, and other naiads

HELICOPTER DAMSELFLY

FAMILY PSEUDOSTIGMATIDAE

Helicopter damselflies are cool to encounter while walking through a tropical rain forest in Central or South America. These giant insects seem to fly in slow motion as they appear in a beam of sunlight through a gap in the tree canopy. When the sunlight hits the damselfly, the yellow spots on the ends of its long, transparent wings seem to bounce up and down.

Damselflies are related to dragonflies, but unlike dragonflies, they close their wings when they come to rest. The helicopter damselfly has a unique diet. It flies up to a spider web and plucks the spider right out of the web. It might even take the spider's wrapped prey too.

These damselflies also visit small bodies of water—in tree holes and in the cup formed by the leaves of certain plants, like tank bromeliads. The female lays her eggs there, and the naiads (nymphs) live in the water, feeding on various insects and even on frog tadpoles.

A female helicopter damselfly, *Megaloprepus caerulatus,* laying her eggs in a tree hole

The male helicopter damselfly is territorial and will defend a tree hole in his territory from other males. A male will not permit a female to lay her eggs in his tree hole unless she mates with him first.

HABITAT	Tropical habitats; naiads in water-filled tree holes and bromeliads
RANGE	Mexico, Central America, and tropical parts of South America

EARWIG

ORDER DERMAPTERA

According to a common myth, earwigs crawl into the ears of people sleeping outdoors, and then burrow into their brains and kill them. Not true!

There are some 1,800 species of earwigs. Their short, leather-like forewings give this order its name, which means "skin wings." At their tail end, many earwigs have two long pincers. The pincers are used during courtship and for capturing prey, defending against predators, and folding and unfolding their membranous hind wings.

After most female insects lay eggs, their parental responsibility to the next generation is over. However, some female earwigs care for their eggs and young nymphs. They clean the eggs regularly to prevent fungal growth, and they defend their young from predators. As the young grow up, they go through four to six molts. The final molt results in an adult.

Earwigs like to hide out during the day. You might find them in compost, at the base of leaves, or in tree holes. Sometimes they go indoors, if they can find a crack in the walls.

FACTS

COMMON NAME	Earwig
SCIENTIFIC NAME	Order: Dermaptera
FOOD	Adult and Nymph: flowers, leaves, fruits, aphids, spiders, insect eggs, mold
SIZE	The common earwig, *Forficula auricularia,* grows up to 0.75 inch (20 mm)
WINGS	Short forewings, membranous hind wings for flying; some species are wingless

HABITAT In soil, crevices, and debris

RANGE The Americas, Africa, Europe, Asia, Australia, and New Zealand

Icebugs have adapted to live in such cold environments that if you put one in your hand, it will cook! The proteins in their bodies break down at room temperature.

FACTS

OTHER COMMON NAMES Ice crawler, rock crawler

SIZE 0.7–1.5 inches (17–38 mm)

WINGS No

SCIENTIFIC NAME Family: Grylloblattidae

FOOD Adult and Nymph: other insects and plant material

ICEBUG

FAMILY GRYLLOBLATTIDAE

You'd think that insects would avoid really cold places. But there are a few that defy expectations—the icebugs. For them, the ideal temperature is close to freezing, between 33.8° to 37.4°F (1 to 3°C), but they can tolerate lower temperatures too. Icebugs are extremophiles—organisms that, along with waterbears and certain bacteria, live under extreme environmental conditions. When it gets too cold for icebugs, they burrow under snow packs, under rocks, and in other places so they don't freeze. Their bodies have a built-in kind of antifreeze that lowers their freezing temperature.

Icebugs are wingless and have chewing mouthparts. They are active at night and can be seen scrambling out onto snow fields to feed on frozen insects.

HABITAT Cold areas, usually in mountains, under rocks, in caves, on leaf litter

RANGE Japan, China, Korea, eastern Siberia, and western North America

STONEFLY

ORDER PLECOPTERA

Stoneflies are poor flyers, so they can't travel very far. As a result, these insects have to come up with creative ways to meet other members of their species.

To find a mate, a male stonefly will drum up some noise—literally. The male produces a series of vibrations, called "drumming," by tapping, rubbing, or scraping his abdomen on a rock or log. Some males even do push-ups!

The drumming vibrations travel through the rock or log and get the attention of any female nearby. If the female is interested, she responds by drumming back. The two stoneflies continue to communicate in this way until they find each other.

The larvae of stoneflies can't survive in polluted waters. So their presence in streams or rivers suggests that the quality of the water is good.

FACTS

COMMON NAME Stonefly		**SCIENTIFIC NAME** Order: Plecoptera	
WINGS Some species are wingless		**SIZE** 0.25–2.0 inches (6–50 mm)	
FOOD Adult: some species feed on pollen, lichen, and nectar / Nymph: plant matter or small aquatic animals, depending on species			

HABITAT   On rocks or logs near rivers and streams

RANGE   Found worldwide except Antarctica

FACTS

OTHER COMMON NAME	Walking leaf	**SCIENTIFIC NAME**	Family: Phylliidae
SIZE	2–4 inches (50–100 mm)	**WINGS**	Yes, but only the hind wings are used by the males to fly
FOOD	Adult and Nymph: leaves		

LEAF INSECT

FAMILY PHYLLIIDAE

Leaf insects are some of the most remarkable examples of camouflage.

Together with the walking sticks, they make up the order Phasmatodea, which comes from the Greek word *phasma*, meaning phantom or ghost.

Leaf insects mimic leaves so convincingly that you can look right at one on a branch and not see that it's an insect. Various species take on the color of live green leaves or dead or dying ones. Most have what looks exactly like leaf veins on their abdomen. Some appear to have bite marks on their "leaf" edges. These insects even sway back and forth, resembling a leaf in the wind.

The oldest known leaf insect fossil is 47 million years old. It was found in Germany.

HABITAT	Tropical forests
RANGE	India to Fiji Islands

CHAN'S MEGASTICK

FAMILY PHASMATIDAE

Chan's megastick is a mega-sized stick insect.

It is the longest known insect in the world, measuring 22.3 inches (567 mm) with its legs outstretched. That's almost two feet! It was named after the person who discovered it. Its body is pencil-thin and resembles a dark green bamboo shoot. With such remarkable camouflage, it can seem invisible to birds and other predators.

Most Chan's megasticks live in tropical and subtropical areas. They sleep during the day and eat leaves at night.

Stick insects generally flick their eggs in the air so the eggs can drop to the ground. The megastick's eggs are unique. They are flat, lightweight and have little wings to help them drift and scatter in the wind.

FACTS

COMMON NAME	Chan's megastick	
SCIENTIFIC NAME	*Phobaeticus chani* / Family: Phasmatidae	
SIZE	With legs outstretched, 22.3 inches (567 mm) /body alone 14.1 inches (358 mm)	
FOOD	Adult and Nymph: leaves	
WINGS	Yes	

Many stick insects can reproduce without mating. The female produces eggs that are clones of herself. In fact, scientists have been unable to find even one male in certain species of stick insects!

HABITAT Rain forest

RANGE State of Sabah on the island of Borneo

Male mole crickets have spade-like forelegs, which they use to dig their specialized burrow. The forelegs are powerful and can scoop out dirt and push it to the surface quickly. From the ground, the cricket's burrow looks like a miniature version of that dug up by the small, furry mammal for which it is named.

FACTS

OTHER COMMON NAME European mole cricket

SCIENTIFIC NAME *Gryllotalpa gryllotalpa* / Family: Gryllotalpidae

SIZE 1.4–1.8 inches (35–46 mm)

WINGS Yes

FOOD Adult: roots and stems of plants; worms; larvae of other insects / Nymph: soil invertebrates and plant material

MOLE CRICKET

FAMILY GRYLLOTALPIDAE

If you hear loud chirping on a spring night, you might be listening to the sound of a mole cricket. Male mole crickets chirp by rubbing two parts of their body together. For instance, the European mole cricket rubs the specialized veins that are on the tip of each of its forewings. These veins are called a "harp."

As the mole cricket plays its harp, the chirping sound travels through the air, and is detected by a female nearby. If she likes the song, she'll find the male and mate with him. Typically, females prefer songs that have a higher pitch. This indicates that the male cricket is larger, and will likely be a more suitable mate.

To ensure that his chirps travel far enough to reach any females in the area, the male mole cricket performs a little trick. It produces its chirps while inside a special burrow. The burrow acts like a megaphone, amplifying the sound of the chirps!

HABITAT	Damp, rich soils; floodplains; vegetable gardens
RANGE	Europe, United States

EASTERN LUBBER

FAMILY ACRIDIDAE

Many grasshoppers rely on their jumping abilities to escape predators. But the eastern lubber isn't a very good hopper. Its large size and short wings make this insect a slow, clumsy mover. Still, the lubber isn't easy prey. It has a few special tricks to ward off enemies.

When eastern lubbers are nymphs (photo below), they move around in large groups. This makes them look like one large insect, which can intimidate some potential predators.

When attacked, the adult lubber sprays out a foamy brown liquid made from a mixture of chemicals and recently digested plant material.

The lubber might also make sound effects when attacked. It pushes air out of tiny holes inside its thorax. The result is a loud hissing sound that can startle some predators.

FACTS

COMMON NAME	Eastern lubber	**SCIENTIFIC NAME**	*Romalea guttata* / Family: Acrididae
SIZE	2.5–3.0 inches (64–76 mm)	**WINGS**	Yes	**FOOD**	Adult and Nymph: plants

The eastern lubber's bright orange, yellow, and black pattern acts as a warning sign. It lets predators know that it's toxic. Predators that don't heed the warning get a bad case of indigestion when they eat the lubber!

HABITAT Woodland and fields

RANGE Southeastern and south-central United States

Unlike most grasshoppers, blue-winged grasshoppers don't make snapping, crackling, or buzzing sounds when in flight.

FACTS

COMMON NAME	Blue-winged grasshopper	**SCIENTIFIC NAME**	*Oedipoda caerulescens* / Family: Acrididae
SIZE	0.6–1.1 inches (15–28 mm)	**WINGS**	Yes
		FOOD	Adult and Nymph: plants such as grasses

BLUE-WINGED GRASSHOPPER

FAMILY ACRIDIDAE

Some grasshoppers use color to confuse their predators.

Take, for instance, the blue-winged grasshopper. At rest, this insect is a mottled brown (photo below). But when it takes flight, the grasshopper's hind wings spread open to reveal a bright shade of blue.

The blue appearance can attract the attention of predators. Some birds may even mistake the airborne grasshopper for a fluttering butterfly. But when it is chased, the grasshopper shuts its wings and drops to the ground. The blue is no longer visible—and neither is the grasshopper to its potential attacker. Camouflaged against the ground, the blue-winged grasshopper can be sitting just a few feet from its predator without being detected!

HABITAT	Dunes, heath, grasslands
RANGE	Europe, North Africa, Asia

GRASSHOPPERS GALLERY

In the order Orthoptera, most of what we call "grasshoppers" have short antennae. The others—katydids, crickets, and wetas—have long antennae, and are sometimes called long-horned grasshoppers because their antennae are longer than their bodies. Grasshopper antennae collect chemical signals in the air and help to locate plants on which the grasshoppers feed.

Many grasshoppers have a knack for jumping great distances. A grasshopper that measures one-inch (25 mm) long can cover 20 times its body length in just one hop.

To jump, grasshoppers rely mainly on special organs located inside the knees of their hind legs. These organs are made of elastic fibers that store energy. When a grasshopper prepares to leap, the energy is released. As a result, its body is propelled forward.

Like many insects, grasshoppers come in different colors. Some are even pink! Set your sights on these six colorful creatures.

Some species of grasshoppers become locusts as adults and seem to appear out of nowhere. They can travel great distances and cause damage to crops wherever they go. The individual shown here is from Honduras.

Some grasshoppers, like this "army hopper," have mottled bodies that help them blend in with their environment.

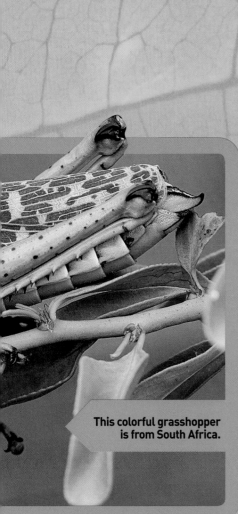

This colorful grasshopper is from South Africa.

The nymphs of the differential grasshopper, like the adults, feed on many different plants, including grasses, soybean, and clover.

When baby grasshoppers, called nymphs, hatch from their eggs, they can sometimes be found gathered together.

Though most grasshoppers are green or brown, some—like this pink nymph—are much brighter. Pink grasshoppers are rare, most likely because they are easy for predators to spot.

CONEHEAD KATYDID

SUBFAMILY COPIPHORINAE

Can you spot the conehead katydid? At first glance, it looks like a leaf. That's because the conehead katydid's appearance helps it to blend in against a leafy background. This grasshopper-like insect usually has a cone on top of its head. In conehead species that live in the grasslands, the cone helps to camouflage the insect among the grasses. In other environments, these pointy cones may help protect the katydid from bats.

At night, conehead katydids can draw a bit of attention to themselves. Some species make loud chirping sounds, and even dance, to attract mates. One species of conehead produces the loudest insect song in North America. It can be heard as far away as a third of a mile.

How do katydids hear each other's songs? The insects have a special organ in each foreleg that works like an ear to pick up sounds.

It's hard to spot this conehead katydid in the wild because it looks exactly like a leaf!

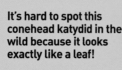

FACTS

COMMON NAME	Conehead katydid	**SCIENTIFIC NAME**	Subfamily: Copiphorinae
SIZE	0.9–2.9 inches (24–74 mm)	**WINGS**	Yes
FOOD	Adult and Nymph: seeds, fruit, and small invertebrates		

Conehead katydids get their common name from the round or pointed cone at the top of their heads. This particular species, *Copiphora rhinoceros*, is known as the rhinoceros spearbearer for obvious reasons.

HABITAT   Rain forests, grasslands

RANGE   Worldwide; mostly tropical and subtropical regions

The praying mantis is the state insect of Connecticut—even though it's not native to the state. The praying mantis is originally from Europe. Experts believe that the insect was accidentally shipped to North America with some nursery plants in 1899.

FACTS

OTHER COMMON NAME   European mantis   **SCIENTIFIC NAME**   *Mantis religiosa* / Family: Mantidae

SIZE   2–3 inches (50–75 mm)   **WINGS**   Yes

FOOD   Adult: insects such as flies, crickets, mosquitoes / Nymph: small insects and, sometimes, each other

PRAYING MANTIS

FAMILY MANTIDAE

The praying mantis is named for its long forelimbs, which the insect holds folded in front of its body as if praying. However, this mantis isn't praying—it's *preying!*

The mantis sits motionless on a plant, waiting for a juicy insect such as a fly or cricket to come by. Usually, the prey has no idea what's about to happen because it can't detect the predator. That's because the mantis's body blends in with the plant it's sitting on.

When the prey is in close range, the mantis strikes. Its front legs shoot out to seize the insect. These legs are covered with spikes, allowing the mantis to get a firm grip on the struggling prey as it begins to chomp away on it.

This praying mantis is sinking its mandibles into a grasshopper.

HABITAT	Meadows, fields, gardens, pastures, and roadsides
RANGE	Europe, North America

91

MANTISES GALLERY

Not all mantises are green or brown like the praying mantis. Depending on the species, these masters of disguise come in many colors, including pink and white, which make them look like flowers. Some species in Africa can change their color. They are bright green in the rainy season, when their environment is lush with green plants. They turn brown in the dry season, when most of these plants shrivel and die. This change of color helps to camouflage them at any time of year.

Most mantises are loners. They can't live with other members of their species because they might eat them!

There are more than 2,400 species of mantises in the world. Here are a few for you to feast your eyes on.

In this photo, the mantis's front legs are raised in a defensive posture.

A flower mantis opens its wings as it prepares to fly.

The forelegs of a praying mantis have sharp spikes. The mantis uses these spikes to pin its prey.

When a mantis feels threatened, it strikes a defensive pose. In this case, it fans out its wings to seem larger—and even more intimidating—than it already is.

A praying mantis's vision plays an important role in hunting. The insect uses its large compound eyes to spot prey, and it can turn its head 180 degrees to see what's happening directly behind it.

This Malaysian orchid mantis can be hard to spot on similarly colored orchids. In this photo, everything that looks like a pink petal is a part of the mantis.

MAGNETIC TERMITE

FAMILY TERMITIDAE

Magnetic termites, like ants and other termites, live together in groups, or colonies. They are social insects, which means colony members perform different tasks. Even the nymphs of some species serve as workers: They help with finding food and maintaining the nest.

The magnetic termite makes mounds up to 13 feet (4 m) tall, and each colony has its own mound. This species of termite got its name from the way it constructs its flattened mound in a north–south direction. The termite has an internal compass—a sense of direction—that helps direct mound-building. In northern Australia, it's quite a sight to see a field full of mounds all oriented in the same direction. The thin shape and alignment of the mounds provides a stable, temperature-controlled structure for the termites to live in, even when their habitat is flooded for part of the year.

Many termites specialize in eating wood and dead plant material. The workers are responsible for digesting the food and then feeding it to the other members of the colony.

Magnetic termites— adults and nymphs

FACTS

OTHER COMMON NAME	Compass termite
SCIENTIFIC NAME	*Amitermes meridionalis* / Family: Termitidae
SIZE	Soldier: 0.16–0.24 inch (4–6 mm)
WINGS	No, for the workers; yes, for the reproductives
FOOD	Adult and Nymph: dead wood and grasses

Aboriginal (native) Australians make a wind instrument from thin tree trunks that are hollowed out by termites. This traditional instrument, the didgeridoo, has been around for about 2,000 years.

HABITAT Seasonally flooded savanna plains

RANGE Northern Australia

FACTS

COMMON NAME Head louse

SCIENTIFIC NAME *Pediculus humanus* / Subspecies: *capitis* / Family: Pediculidae

SIZE 0.04–0.12 inch (1–3 mm)

WINGS No

FOOD Adult and Nymph: human blood

HEAD LOUSE

FAMILY PEDICULIDAE

Try not to scratch yourself as you read this page. If you're unlucky enough to get head lice, don't be embarrassed. You're in good company. Many people have been getting them for thousands of years. Just take measures to get rid of them as soon as possible.

Head lice are flightless insects that live exclusively on blood from people's scalps. A related subspecies (body lice) lives in clothes and feeds on other parts of a person's body. Head lice don't cause disease, but they are annoying and hard to get rid of. Without wings, head lice transfer from one person to another, usually by head-to-head contact. The adult louse glues its eggs, called nits, to individual strands of a person's hair near the scalp. The newly hatched nymphs look like miniature adults and also feed on the scalp.

Girls are more likely to get head lice than boys or adults are. Scientists are studying the reasons why.

Around the world, people turn to nit-picking as one of the most effective ways of controlling a head louse infestation. Treatments with vegetable or olive oil and nit-removing combs are also popular.

A mother in India nit-picking her child's scalp

HABITAT	People's heads
RANGE	Worldwide

97

THRIPS

ORDER THYSANOPTERA

Some thrips have a bad reputation. They can be crop pests, transmitting plant viruses and leaving scars on fruit, leaves, and flowers. But thrips do a lot of good, too. There are species that are predators of other insects and mites that damage crops. And thrips are major pollinators of certain tropical rain forest trees.

In Malaysia, Indonesia, and the Philippines, many of the tallest rain forest trees, called "dipterocarps," produce huge displays of flowers (photo below), but at irregular intervals of two to ten years. Dependent on the weather, they will flower only when the conditions are right—and when they do, it's spectacular. The main pollinators of these trees are thrips. They crawl around in the trees' flowers and get covered in pollen.

These thrips reproduce very fast. Their life cycle is complete in eight days. In short order, their increasing numbers are enough to fill vast canopies of flowering trees.

Most thrips are so small they're hard to see. They like to get together in groups in tight places. This has caused lots of trouble for people with smoke detectors in the UK. The thrips gather inside the smoke detectors and set off the automatic alarm. False alarms due to thrips cost one fire and rescue service $17,450 (11,000 pounds) in one year.

FACTS

OTHER COMMON NAMES	Thunderfly, thunderbug	**SCIENTIFIC NAME**	Order: Thysanoptera
SIZE	0.02–0.55 inch (0.5–14 mm)	**WINGS**	Yes, feathery
FOOD	Adult and Nymph: plants, flowers, mites, insects, and fungal spores		

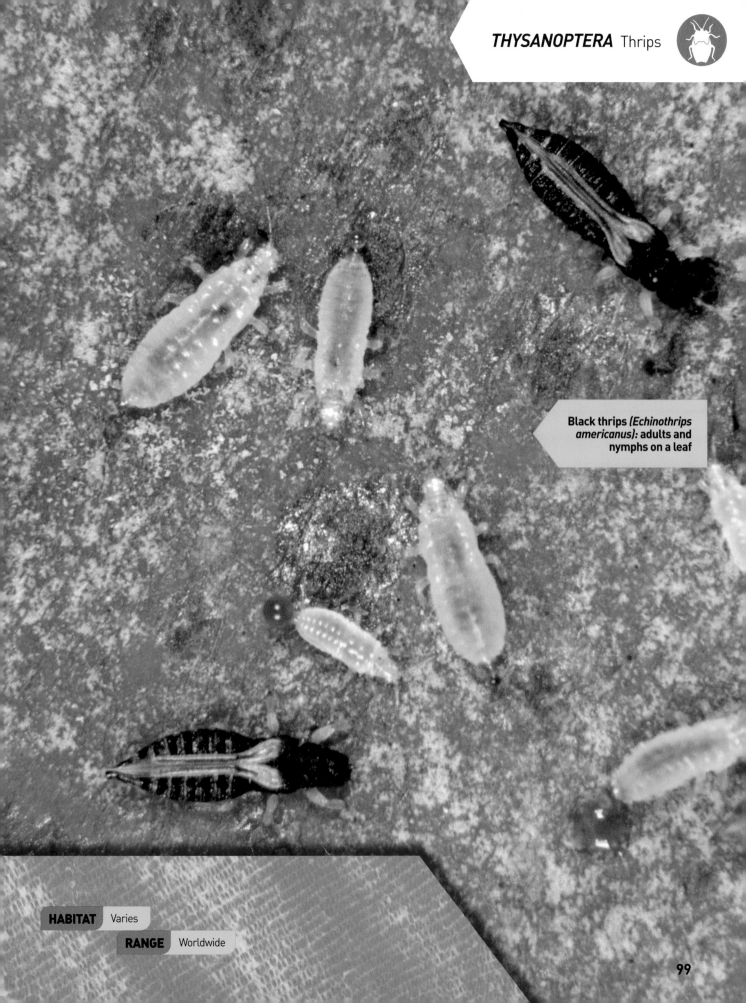

Black thrips *(Echinothrips americanus)*: adults and nymphs on a leaf

HABITAT	Varies
RANGE	Worldwide

FACTS

OTHER COMMON NAMES Yellow Monday, blue moon, chocolate soldier, and masked devil

WINGS Yes

SCIENTIFIC NAME *Cyclochila australasiae* / Family: Cicadidae

SIZE 1.6 inches (40 mm) long, 4.3–5 inches (110–130 mm) wingspan

FOOD Adult: plant sap / Nymph: juices from acacia and eucalyptus roots

GREEN GROCER

FAMILY CICADIDAE

You might not always see cicadas, but you can definitely hear them. The green grocer from the east coast of Australia is one of the loudest cicadas of all. It annoys human residents with its ear-shattering love songs every summer. Green is the predominant color of the adult cicadas. However, they come in other colors as well, depending on their diet and on the temperature under which the nymphs were raised.

The nymphs live underground, feeding on plant roots for about seven years. They emerge as adults in summer, and within a few short weeks, they mate, lay eggs, and die.

Cicadas are widespread in temperate and tropical parts of the world with some 2,500 known species, each having its own song. They cling to tree trunks and limbs and suck sap with their long proboscis.

The cicada hunter wasp *(Exeirus lateritius)* flies up to a green grocer or another type of cicada, stings it, and then drags it to its underground catacombs. There, the wasp lays an egg on the cicada so that its larva will have fresh food to feed on.

HABITAT Where this species can find their host plants

RANGE Southeast coast of Australia

PERIODICAL CICADA

FAMILY CICADIDAE

Periodical cicadas are among the longest-lived insects in North America. The nymphs live underground sucking juices from tree roots for either thirteen or seventeen years, depending on the species. When they are ready, they tunnel to the surface, emerging all together, in spectacular numbers. Then they climb up trees or any vertical surface, and molt to become winged adults. They slide out of their old exoskeleton in the evening and spend the night filling out their new wings and hardening their new exoskeleton.

The males sing in large groups to attract females. Each of the species has its own call and some are extremely loud. A male will switch to a unique courtship song when he approaches a female. The two will mate if the female responds favorably to his song. Then the female cuts slits in tree branches and lays her eggs inside. When the little nymphs hatch out, they fall to the ground and burrow down to the tree roots, not to be seen again for many years.

A periodical cicada transforming into an adult. Its crumpled wings have yet to fill out, and its body will darken and harden.

FACTS

COMMON NAME	Periodical cicada	SCIENTIFIC NAME	*Magicicada* (7 species) / Order: Hemiptera
SIZE	*M. septendecim* is up to 1.5 inches (38 mm) long		WINGS	Yes
FOOD	Adult: plant sap / Nymph: juices from tree roots		

Periodical cicadas are very nutritious. They are high in protein and low in fat. On years with a huge bonanza of periodical cicadas, dogs and cats often eat so many, they get sick. Many wild animals eat them too—as do people! Have you ever heard of a cicada pizza?

HABITAT   Forests; older neighborhoods with large, old trees

RANGE   Eastern United States

CICADAS GALLERY

There are about 2,500 species of cicadas around the world. These bugs range in size from 0.8 to 2 inches (20 to 50 mm). They often have transparent, or see-through, wings with veins, as well as large eyes.

Members of a cicada population typically hatch from their eggs at the same time. After becoming adults, thousands of cicadas can be seen feeding on tree sap. This behavior often gets cicadas mistaken for locusts, a type of short-horned grasshopper with a tendency to travel in swarms. However, cicadas are more closely related to spittlebugs and leafhoppers (see pp. 128–129 and 250–251).

You'll learn more about cicadas on these pages.

Like all insects, cicadas have six jointed legs. The joints are softer than the insect's exoskeleton—and bendable. This makes movement easier.

This dog-day cicada recently finished molting (shedding) its nymphal exoskeleton. As cicada nymphs grow, they molt several times.

Cicadas have water-repellent wings, which also makes them self-cleaning. When dew forms on the wings, the drops slide off, taking with them any unwanted particles—such as pollen.

A cicada's tubelike mouthpart, which is tucked beneath its head, is its proboscis. Cicadas like those of the *Tibicen* genus, shown here, use these mouthparts to pierce and feed on plants.

A cicada has three small eyes, called ocelli, located between two larger compound eyes. The ocelli help the cicada detect changes in light.

After cicadas molt, they leave behind shell-like "skins." These exoskeletons, discovered on a tree trunk, belonged to 17-year cicadas.

A bedbug feeding on a person's arm. Its red abdomen is full of its blood meal.

FACTS

COMMON NAME	Bedbug	**SCIENTIFIC NAME**	*Cimex lectularius* / Family: Cimicidae
SIZE	0.16–0.20 inch (4–5 mm) long	**WINGS**	Yes: tiny, useless forewings, no hind wings
		FOOD	Adult and Nymph: blood meals

BEDBUG

FAMILY CIMICIDAE

Bedbugs are parasites found throughout the world. They rely on stealth to snatch a blood meal from a human host. By day they hide out in snug places like along mattress edges, but at night, when their human host is asleep, they venture out.

The bugs are attracted to the host's exhaled carbon dioxide and body heat. A hungry bedbug has a flattened abdomen that fills out like a blimp as it feeds. People don't feel when bedbugs feed, but a rash can develop—similar to mosquito bites. Bedbugs can't fly, but they easily hitch a ride to new locations in luggage, on pets, and on clothing.

If a human host isn't available and conditions are right, bedbug larvae can wait a long time for their next blood meal—up to a few months; the adults can wait even longer—up to a year or so!

Specially trained detection dogs are often used to sniff out bedbugs in places where they have become pests—mainly in hotels, apartment buildings, and schools.

Scanning electron microscope photo of a bedbug

HABITAT Snug hiding places in human habitations

RANGE Worldwide

PEANUT BUG

FAMILY FULGORIDAE

The peanut bug gets its name from the shape of its head. From afar, it looks like an unshelled peanut. But on closer inspection it looks a lot like the head of a cartoon crocodile with a toothy grin! The peanut bug sits on tree trunks and branches and drinks sap with its long needle-like proboscis.

The most well-known of three peanut bug species is found in Central and South America. Like all peanut bugs, this species is visible on tree trunks, but it has several ways of defending itself from predators. Its mottled color makes it camouflaged from a distance. When disturbed, the peanut bug flashes large eyespots on its hind wings, giving the appearance of something large and scary. And if that doesn't work, it sprays a substance with a foul odor. Its head might also frighten some predators.

FACTS

OTHER COMMON NAMES	Peanut head, peanut head bug, machaca, alligator bug
SCIENTIFIC NAME	*Fulgora laternaria* / Family: Fulgoridae
SIZE	About 3 inches (76 mm) long
WINGS	Yes
FOOD	Adult and Nymph: tree sap

The "peanut head" is actually a long, hollow bulge at the end of the bug's head (like an inflated balloon). The bug's eyes are right behind the hollow structure.

HABITAT Forests

RANGE Central and South America

Some treehoppers live in groups with the mother watching over her nymphs. If a small predator pesters the nymphs, they vibrate to call their mom. She comes to their rescue and confronts the predator, vibrating her wings and kicking it off the plant with her specialized hind legs.

FACTS

COMMON NAME Treehopper

SIZE 0.08–1.2 inches (2–30 mm)

SCIENTIFIC NAME Families: Aetalionidae, Melizoderidae, and Membracidae

WINGS Yes

FOOD Adult and Nymph: plant sap

TREE-HOPPER

FAMILIES AETALIONIDAE, MELIZODERIDAE, AND MEMBRACIDAE

Treehoppers win the prize for the most imaginative variety of bug body shapes. They can resemble leaves, thorns, ants, and even helicopters. There are some 3,500 species. Many have a pronotum—a part of the thorax—that is extended to form a hood, horn, or other elaborate sculpture over its body. Treehoppers can be easy to find on small branches, where they pierce the stem to drink sap, although some are well-camouflaged.

They communicate with others of their species by vibrating. The vibrations travel through their host plant and are picked up by their neighbors. These sounds can communicate alarm, discovery, or courtship.

Treehoppers drink a lot of plant sap and expel the excess as sugary droplets called honeydew. In a mutualistic relationship, ants drink the sweet honeydew secretions, and, in turn, protect the treehoppers from predators.

The shape of the pronotum of this treehopper species, *Bocydium globlare,* is highly unusual. Scientists aren't sure if its pronotum serves a purpose.

HABITAT   Plant stems

RANGE   All regions of the world except New Zealand, Madagascar, and Antarctica

111

COCHINEAL SCALE INSECT

FAMILY DACTYLOPIIDAE

Some scale insects look like their name suggests—like little flattened scales. Many are covered in white wax secreted from their bodies.

When a scale insect hatches from its egg, the emerging nymph is called a crawler. In some species, females lose their legs after the first molt and become permanently attached to their host plant. Males keep their legs, and depending on the species, they may or may not have wings as adults. As adults, they only live a day or two, during which they search for females in order to mate.

Although some scale insects are considered pests and harm crops, the cochineal species is valued. Cochineal scale insects cluster together and drink sap from prickly-pear cactus pads. Their particular diet allows them to produce a red pigment that can be turned into a dye called carmine. Carmine from cochineal scale insects was traditionally used for coloring fabrics, but today it's used in cosmetics and food coloring.

In the late 1700s, a ship captain brought infected prickly-pear cacti from Brazil to Australia in order to start a cochineal dye industry. However, the scale insects died out, and the prickly-pear cactus spread to cover some 100,000 square miles (259,000 sq km) in eastern Australia. In the 1920s, a cactus-feeding moth was introduced to control the runaway cactus population.

FACTS

COMMON NAME	Cochineal scale insect
SCIENTIFIC NAME	*Dactylopius coccus* / Family: Dactylopiidae
SIZE	About 0.2 inch (5 mm) long
WINGS	Male: one pair / Female: no
FOOD	Adult and Nymph: *Opuntia* (prickly-pear) cactus

White waxy patches on prickly-pear cactus pads are a giveaway that cochineal scale insects live here.

A cluster of large female cochineal scales attached to a cactus pad

HABITAT   Arid deserts

RANGE   Central and South America; desert areas of U.S. and Mexico; introduced to Australia

FACTS

OTHER COMMON NAME   Cotton harlequin bug

SCIENTIFIC NAME   *Tectocoris diophthalmus* / Family: Scutelleridae

FOOD   Adult and Nymph: plant juices

SIZE   Up to 0.8 inch (20 mm)

WINGS   Yes

HIBISCUS HARLEQUIN BUG

FAMILY SCUTELLERIDAE

The hibiscus harlequin bug is a type of jewel bug—
a group of shield-shaped insects known for their bright, metallic
colors. The male (left) is iridescent blue and red; the female, bright
orange with sparkly blue markings. These markings may serve
to warn that they are toxic and therefore unsafe to eat.

The bug's colors also help the insect protect its young.
After the female hibiscus harlequin lays her eggs, she
perches on them. Her bright shield is clearly visible to
wasps and other predators that would attack her eggs
if they were unattended.

The female hibiscus harlequin continues to tend her
brood after they hatch. She keeps an eye on the
nymphs as they scoot from one plant to another to
feed. Only when the nymphs are capable of taking care
of themselves does the mother leave.

Jewel bugs
feed on plants the
way spiders feed on
insects. They inject saliva
with digestive enzymes
into a plant, and then suck
up the juices.

HABITAT Wide-ranging (cities, farms, and coastal areas)

RANGE Parts of Australia, New Guinea, and some Pacific islands

115

JEWEL BUGS GALLERY

Jewel bugs are true bugs in the family Scutelleridae. They lay their eggs in clusters on plants. After the embryos inside the eggs mature, they wiggle around until eventually they push their way out through the top of the egg. They emerge as nymphs, and then often remain together in their cluster, spending much of their time feeding on plants. Some experts believe that this clustering behavior makes the group look larger—and more intimidating to predators.

Jewel bugs typically have bright iridescent colors, such as green, red, purple, pink, and blue. Their iridescence is not caused by pigments, but by how light interacts with the surface of their bodies.

The shiny creatures shown here are just some of the amazing jewel bugs found around the world. Check them out!

Like a stink bug (see pp. 118–119), a jewel bug can release foul-smelling chemicals from the sides of its thorax when threatened.

The jewel bug's shield is called a scuttellum. It's formed by the last section of the insect's thorax and it extends down to cover the abdomen. This makes jewel bugs different from beetles, whose cover is formed by hardened forewings.

Although most jewel bugs are harmless to plants, some species have been known to cause great damage to crops.

Color and pattern not only varies among different species of jewel bugs, but it also changes as a jewel bug develops.

While feeding, jewel bugs inject enzymes from their saliva into the plant. This helps liquefy the plant so that the jewel bug can suck it up.

117

STINK BUG

FAMILY PENTATOMIDAE

Get a whiff of this: When stink bugs feel threatened by a predator, they let out a nasty, foul-smelling liquid. The odor is so bad, it's often enough to drive some predators away. It's no wonder why these critters are named as they are. The stink bug's smelly liquid is a mixture of compounds that are produced by glands located in the insect's body. In the adult bug, the glands are found in its thorax, while nymphs possess the glands in their abdomen.

Stink bugs don't just pose a problem to predators; they can also be a nuisance to people. Each year, these bugs cause millions of dollars worth of damage to crops. They also get into people's homes. And if you think that we aren't immune to the bug's stinkiness, think again. Many people who accidentally step on the bug smell a skunk-like odor. *Eew.*

When the stink bug releases its liquid, it flaps its wings to help spread the odor. This takes a lot of energy, so it isn't always the bug's first line of defense. Sometimes, the stink bug produces a sound to startle its predators. It makes the sound by rubbing together its legs and wings.

FACTS

COMMON NAME	Stink bug
SCIENTIFIC NAME	Family: Pentatomidae
SIZE	About 0.75 inch (19 mm)
WINGS	Yes
FOOD	Adult and Nymph: mainly plant sap; some species eat insects

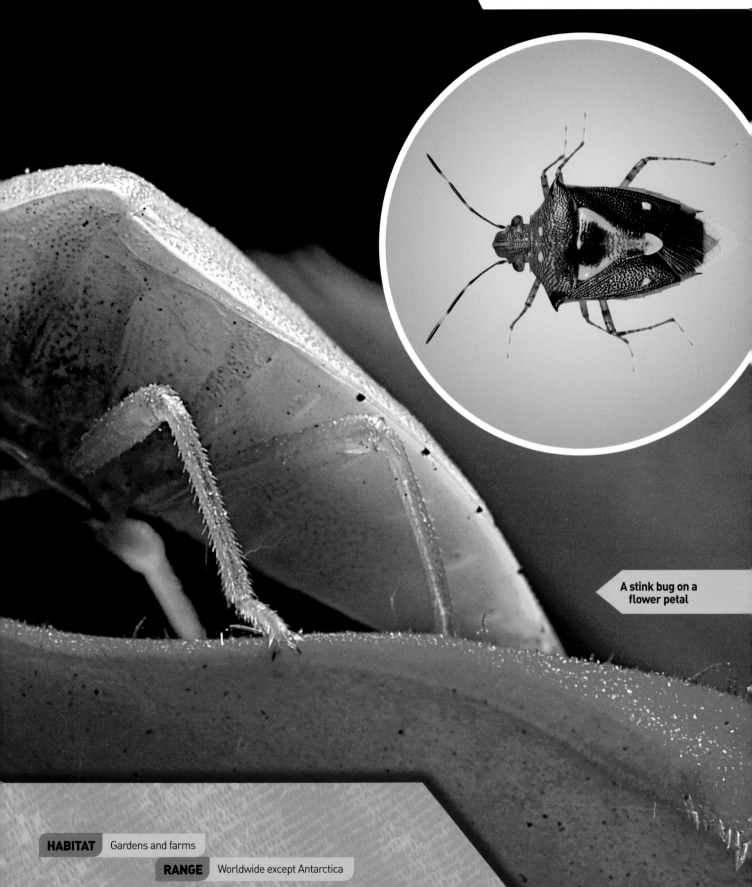

A stink bug on a flower petal

HABITAT	Gardens and farms
RANGE	Worldwide except Antarctica

119

This wheel bug—a type of assassin bug—plunges its beak into a bee. The wheel bug is so named because part of its thorax is shaped like a wheel.

FACTS

COMMON NAME	Assassin bug	**SCIENTIFIC NAME**	Family: Reduviidae
SIZE	Some species can grow more than 1.0 inch (25 mm)	**WINGS**	Yes
FOOD	Adult: insects / Nymph: dead insects; sometimes eats other members of its species		

ASSASSIN BUG

FAMILY REDUVIIDAE

Unlike many bugs, which only kill prey that wander into their immediate territory, assassin bugs actively seek out their victims. How do they do it? That depends on the type of assassin bug.

The thread-legged assassin bug (subfamily Emesinae) preys on web-building spiders. When it comes across a web, it plucks the threads. This mimics the movement of prey caught in the web. The spider, thinking it has caught a meal, scurries over—and ends up becoming a meal itself!

One assassin bug (*Ptilocerus ochraceus*) has tufts of red hair on its abdomen, which attracts ants. These tufts of hair secrete a poisonous fluid. When the ants lick the fluid, they become paralyzed—an easy lunch for the bug.

Millipede assassin bugs prefer to hunt in groups. They team up to take down millipedes that are often ten times their size!

An ant-eating assassin bug, the *Acanthaspis petax*, piles the corpses of its victims onto its body. This makes it look a lot larger than it is, and thus intimidates some would-be predators.

HABITAT Most often on shrubs and dense vegetation

RANGE Worldwide

121

GIANT WATER BUG

FAMILY BELOSTOMATIDAE

As its name suggests, the giant water bug is one big bug. Some species can grow up to 4 inches (100 mm) long. That's longer than the width of an average human hand!

The bugs have a hefty appetite to match their large size. One species, *Kirkaldyia deyrolli*, has been seen eating a pond turtle in Japan!

A giant water bug relies on its powerful forelegs to snag its prey. It then uses its sharp beak to pierce the victim's body and inject it with a powerful toxin that breaks down tissue. Once the prey's tissue has been liquefied, the giant water bug can begin to feed.

The females of certain giant water bugs glue their eggs on the backs of males. The males then care for the eggs until they hatch.

FACTS

OTHER COMMON NAMES	Toe-biter, electric-light bug
SCIENTIFIC NAME	Family: Belostomatidae
SIZE	Up to 4 inches (100 mm)
WINGS	Yes
FOOD	Adult: bugs, small fish, frogs, and salamanders / Nymph: small aquatic invertebrates

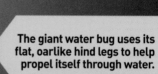

The giant water bug uses its flat, oarlike hind legs to help propel itself through water.

HABITAT	Clear, freshwater streams and ponds
RANGE	Worldwide, but most diverse in tropics

There are 46 known species of insects that belong to the water strider family. Only five species of the water strider family live in the open ocean; *Halobates sericeus,* shown here, is one of them.

FACTS

COMMON NAME	Sea skater	**SCIENTIFIC NAME**	*Halobates sericeus* / Family: Gerridae	
SIZE	0.13–0.24 inch (3.4–6.0 mm)	**WINGS**	Yes	**FOOD** Adult and Nymph: plankton

WATER STRIDER

FAMILY GERRIDAE

Sea skaters are a type of water strider—insects that are able to move easily across the water's surface. While most water striders are found in freshwater habitats, sea skaters live almost exclusively in the ocean, where they feed on tiny organisms called plankton.

So how are sea skaters able to stay on the water's surface without sinking? It has a lot to do with their legs.

The sea skater's legs and body are covered with layers of tiny needle-shaped hairs. Air gets trapped in the spaces between these hairs and forms an air cushion. This keeps the water strider's body from ever getting wet, and thus keeps the bug above the water's surface.

Like all insects, sea skaters have three pairs of legs. Each pair has a different function. The front legs are used to support the body while at rest, to grasp and hold prey, and, in males, to hold on to the female while mating. The middle legs help propel the body through water, while the back legs help steer.

Although they live on the surface of the ocean, sea skaters need to lay their eggs on a solid object, such as a floating coconut or wood debris.

HABITAT	Ocean surface
RANGE	Pacific Ocean

EGGPLANT LACE BUG

FAMILY TINGIDAE

Eggplant lace bugs look nothing like eggplants. Instead, they have striking wings and a pronotum (part of the thorax) that resembles lace. The bug got the name "eggplant" in 1913, after it harmed many eggplant crops in Virginia.

The bugs may have a bad reputation where crops are concerned, but they have a good reputation in the parenting department. The female eggplant lace bug is a very attentive parent. She guards her clutch of eggs closely, leaving only for brief periods to feed. After her nymphs break free from their eggs, she continues to care for them. Sometimes, she'll lead them from one leaf to another to feed. During this migration, she scoots from the front of the group to the back, making sure that all the nymphs are together and heading in the right direction. If she spots a straggler, she gently nudges it back into the group with her antennae.

Eggplants are one kind of plant that eggplant lace bugs feed on.

Lace bugs are plant feeders, and can spend their entire lives on the same plant. They prefer to hang out on the underside of leaves, where they suck up sap from the plant's tissue.

COMMON NAME	Eggplant lace bug	SCIENTIFIC NAME	*Gargaphia solani* / Family: Tingidae
SIZE	0.16 inch (4 mm)	WINGS	Yes
FOOD	Adult and Nymph: liquids sucked from tomatoes, potatoes, eggplant		

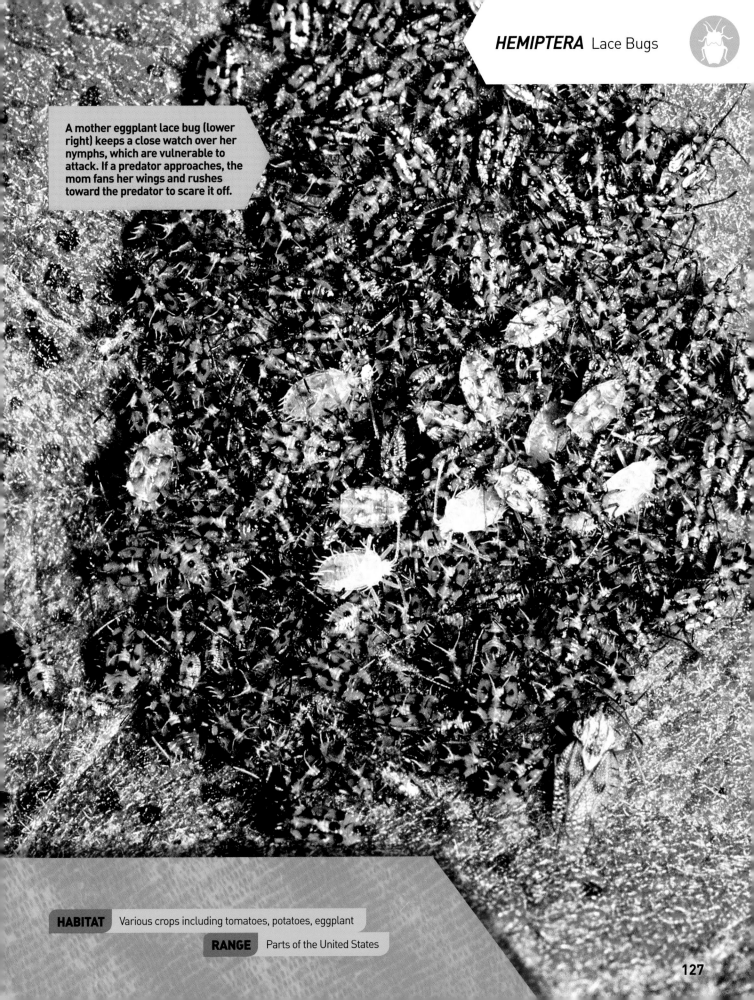

A mother eggplant lace bug (lower right) keeps a close watch over her nymphs, which are vulnerable to attack. If a predator approaches, the mom fans her wings and rushes toward the predator to scare it off.

HABITAT Various crops including tomatoes, potatoes, eggplant

RANGE Parts of the United States

FACTS

OTHER COMMON NAME Froghopper

SCIENTIFIC NAME Superfamily: Cercopoidea

SIZE 0.125–0.5 inch (4–13 mm) long

WINGS Yes

FOOD Adult and Nymph: sap from grasses and other herbs

SPITTLE-BUG

SUPERFAMILY CERCOPOIDEA

Don't be grossed out if you see a ball of foamy "spit" coating the stalk of a plant. A young spittlebug may be nestled inside!

After spittlebug nymphs hatch from their eggs, they feed on plant sap. The nymphs take in more sap than they need for food. The extra sap gets mixed with a special substance inside the spittlebug's body, and it's then released from an opening at the tip of its abdomen. When this mixture is combined with air, it turns into a frothy blob that looks a lot like spit.

The nymph lives inside this spitlike ball until it becomes an adult. The spit keeps the nymph's body moist, and it also helps conceal the young bug from predators.

Adult spittlebugs are known as froghoppers because of their incredible jumping skills. Froghoppers can leap more than 2 feet (60 cm) into the air. That's as much as 100 times their body length.

| **HABITAT** | Mainly grasslands and garden plants |
| **RANGE** | Worldwide |

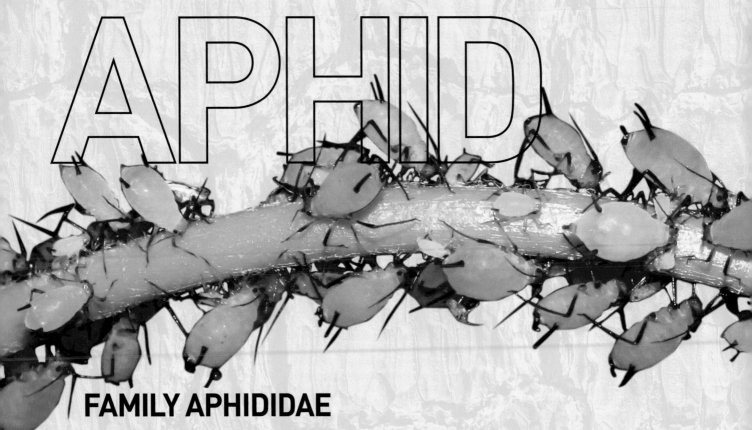

APHID

FAMILY APHIDIDAE

When it comes to surviving in the wild, it's who you know that counts. Few insects know this better than the aphid.

Aphids are tiny plant-feeding insects that rarely measure more than 0.4 inches (10 mm) long. Their small size can make them vulnerable to predators, which is why some species rely on the help of others to get by.

One North American species, *Pemphigus obesinymphae*, raises an army of daughters who defend the colony. If a predator, such as a lacewing larva, threatens the colony, the soldier daughters swarm over it. They pierce the predator with their sharp mouthparts, harming and sometimes killing it.

Other species, such as the woolly alder aphid *(Prociphilus tessellates)* rely on the help of ants to ward off their attackers. Do the ants get anything in return for their bodyguard duties? Yes! The aphids excrete a sugary liquid called honeydew that the ants feed on.

FACTS

OTHER COMMON NAMES	Greenbug, greenfly, and plant louse	**SCIENTIFIC NAME**	Family: Aphididae
FOOD	Adult and Nymph: plant sap of particular plants	**SIZE**	0.04–0.4 inch (1–10 mm) long
WINGS	Winged and wingless forms are found in many species		

Aphids are sometimes called "ant cows" because their relationship to ants is similar to that of cattle to humans. Ants tend their aphids and feed on their honeydew just as humans tend cattle and feed on their milk!

HABITAT	Trees, shrubs, and garden plants
RANGE	Worldwide, but occur most often in temperate zones

Monarch pupa

Mosquito larvae and pupae underwater. The pupae have the big heads.

Close-up of a ladybug larva

Peablue butterfly

The larva of a *Dysphania militaris* moth crawling on a branch

COMPLETE
METAMORPHOSIS

Male Hercules beetle pupa

INSECT ORDERS

Young insects, called larvae, undergo complete metamorphosis, which means they change dramatically as they develop and grow. A wriggling larva hardly looks like the winged adult that it will become. Not until it is almost ready to emerge from its pupa do its wings become visible.

Here you'll find a list of all the different orders of insects with complete metamorphosis. The scientific name for the order is noted below the common name. The figures below it are estimates of the number of insects in that order that have already been named and described. That number is constantly changing. Many additional insect specimens are in museum collections around the world waiting to be described, and many more have yet to be collected. Also, scientists sometimes change the name of an order to reflect new information they discover about the insects within in. To find out about the different species within an order, just turn to the page number noted.

BUTTERFLIES AND MOTHS
Lepidoptera
leh · pih · DOP · ter · uh
About 174,000 species
pp. 216–247

BEETLES
Coleoptera
coh · lee · OP · ter · uh
About 400,000 species
pp. 136–167

ANTS, BEES, SAWFLIES, AND WASPS
Hymenoptera
high · men · OP · ter · uh
About 130,000 species
pp. 174–199

FLIES
Diptera
DIP · ter · uh
About 120,000 species
pp. 202–213

CADDISFLIES
Trichoptera
tri · COP · ter · uh
About 13,000 species
pp. 214–215

LACEWINGS, ANTLIONS, OWL-FLIES, MANTID-FLIES, AND SPOONWINGS
Neuroptera
NUR · OP · ter · uh
About 6,000 species
pp. 170–173

FLEAS
Siphonaptera
sigh · fun · APP · ter · uh
About 2,000 species
pp. 200–201

Ladybug

ALDERFLIES, DOBSONFLIES, AND FISHFLIES
Megaloptera
meg · uh · LOP · ter · uh
About 300 species
pp. 168–169

There are three orders with insects that undergo complete metamorphosis that aren't included in the profiles that start on page 136. They are:

TWISTED-WING PARASITES
Strepsiptera
strep · SIP · ter · uh
About 600 species of unusual parasites that feed on other insects. Males have twisted wings as adults, and the females of most species lack wings and legs.

SCORPIONFLIES AND HANGING FLIES
Mecoptera
meh · COP · ter · uh
About 550 species of predatory, winged insects with long, slender bodies

SNAKEFLIES
Raphidioptera
ruh · fid · ee · OP · ter · uh
About 210 species of predatory, winged insects, with an elongated thorax that looks like a neck

LADYBUG

FAMILY COCCINELLIDAE

Don't be misled by the common name "ladybug."

Ladybugs are not true bugs (Hemiptera) but are instead beetles. There are more than 5,000 species in the family, all with dome-shaped bodies. Both adults and larvae are voracious predators, eating many aphids and scale insects (see pp. 130 and 112) found on plants. During the winter, they hibernate on the warmer south side of trees and buildings. If they can, they go indoors.

As predators, ladybugs control populations of aphids and scale insects that may damage gardens and crops. They in turn have their own predators, like birds, spiders, and some insects. But they have a few defenses against them: Ladybugs taste bad, they can release a foul odor, and they can play dead.

Their average life span is about a year.

Ladybug eating an aphid

FACTS

OTHER COMMON NAMES Ladybird, ladybird beetle, lady beetle **SCIENTIFIC NAME** Family: Coccinellidae

SIZE 0.06–0.4 inch (1–10 mm) long **WINGS** Yes (their forewings are hardened wing covers and their hind wings are for flying)

FOOD Adult and Larva: aphids and scale insects. Adults also eat nectar, pollen, fungi, and honeydew.

Ladybugs are not just female, despite their name, and you can't tell their age by the number of spots on their backs, which is a common myth. But the number of spots does help to identify the species of ladybug.

HABITAT Gardens, trees, shrubs, fields, beaches, and homes

RANGE Worldwide

137

FACTS

OTHER COMMON NAME	Sweet potato leaf beetle	**FOOD**	Adult and Larva: morning glories
SCIENTIFIC NAME	*Charidotella sexpunctata* / Family: Chrysomelidae	**SIZE**	0.20–0.28 inch (5–7 mm) lo
		WINGS	Yes (their forewings are hardened wing covers and their hind wings a

GOLDEN TORTOISE BEETLE

FAMILY CHRYSOMELIDAE

Tortoise beetles look like they have an upside-down bowl over their backs, legs, and head. The bowl is actually their front wings and part of their thorax. It protects them so that predators, like ants, can't grab hold of them.

The golden tortoise beetle is named for its golden, jewel-like appearance on morning glory leaves, their preferred food. However, the bug isn't always golden. It can change its colors. The color change depends on the amount of fluids between layers inside their wings. The fluid is controlled by microscopic valves.

This color change once fooled scientists into believing that they were observing different species of beetles, not one. They even gave the beetle different names.

The larvae of the golden tortoise beetle have an effective way of defending themselves. They have a long, forklike extension at the end of their abdomen that holds large gobs of feces. When they hold this extension (called a fecal parasol) over their bodies, predators ignore them.

HABITAT Found on morning glories

RANGE North America

139

TORTOISE BEETLES GALLERY

Tortoise beetles range in size from 0.2 to 0.4 inch (5 to 10 mm) long. In addition to morning glory leaves, they like to eat the leaves of sweet potato, bindweed, and other plants in the same family.

There are more than 3,000 species of tortoise beetles. They live all over the world. Many come in bright, shimmery colors such as gold, red, and green. Some colors are caused by pigmented liquids inside the outer part of the insect's body. These liquids can also help change a tortoise beetle's colors.

In addition to their protective shells, some tortoise beetles are known for their great parenting skills. After laying their eggs, most female tortoise beetles watch over their brood to protect them from predators. The adult beetles may even remain with their young after they hatch.

Here are six more species of tortoise beetles for you to discover.

This tortoise beetle lifts its hardened elytra (forewings) and spreads its back wings in order to fly.

Many tortoise beetles have jewel-like shells, as shown here. The shell covers all parts of the beetle, except for its antennae.

This female tortoise beetle closely guards her tightly packed eggs. She will protect them from predators such as ants and wasps.

Tortoise beetles typically hatch, feed, and mate on the same plant.

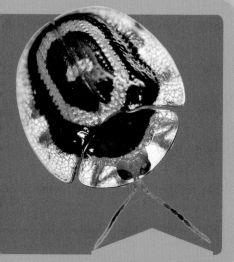

Like other tortoise beetles, the target tortoise beetle from the Amazonian rain forest can clamp itself tightly to a leaf for protection.

This tortoise beetle looks like a crab from this angle. Its head and antennae are clearly visible. Like all insects, tortoise beetles use their antennae to help sense their environment.

VIOLIN BEETLE

FAMILY CARABIDAE

Violin beetles live upside down on the underside of shelf fungi and under tree bark in the tropical rain forests of Southeast Asia. They get their name from the violin-like shape of their body. Their flattened shape allows them to hunt invertebrates in cramped spaces. Having long legs lets them chase down their prey quickly.

A rounded notch on their elytra (front wings) provides an opening for them to extend a pair of turrets (projections) on their abdomen. They can aim the turrets toward an enemy and squirt it with a painful acid. The acid is known to be so strong that it can paralyze a person's hand for a day or more.

Violin beetles dig a chamber in shelf fungi to lay their eggs and provide a home for their larvae as they grow up.

The violin beetle is in the huge family of "ground beetles." It's one of more than 40,000 known species. Although the family is known as ground beetles, many are found in tree canopies, especially in the rain forest.

The violin beetle has been depicted on postage stamps in several countries, demonstrating pride in this iconic insect.

FACTS

COMMON NAME	Violin beetle	**SCIENTIFIC NAME**	*Mormolyce* / Family: Carabidae
SIZE	1.5–4.0 inches (40–100 mm)	**WINGS**	Yes (their forewings are hardened wing covers and their hind wings are for flying)
FOOD	Adult: invertebrates such as insect larvae and snails / Larva: small invertebrates		

HABITAT Under bark, and in bracket fungi

RANGE Southeast Asia

Don't try this at home!
A scientist demonstrates what
happens when you aggravate
a bombardier beetle.

FACTS

COMMON NAME Bombardier beetle

SCIENTIFIC NAME *Pheropsophus jessoensis* / Family: Carabidae

SIZE 0.4 inch (10 mm)

WINGS Yes (their forewings are hardened wing covers and their hind wings are for flying)

FOOD Adult: smaller insects than the larva eats / Larva: small insects

BOMBARDIER BEETLE

FAMILY CARABIDAE

Measuring only 0.4 inch (10 mm) long, the bombardier beetle may not seem like much of a threat. But if you get too close, look out! The beetle shoots out a boiling-hot, skin-blistering liquid.

The liquid is formed from a mix of chemical compounds in a pair of reservoirs in the beetle's abdomen. The beetle can force the chemicals into a reaction chamber at the tip of its abdomen when it's alarmed. There the chemicals react with enzymes to make the boiling liquid.

When the beetle feels threatened, it swivels its abdomen in the direction of its target and shoots the hot liquid. The beetle can aim forward and backward, and side to side, so there is no escape for its attacker.

Some bombardier beetle species are able to fly. But before the beetle can take off, it must open its wing casings and then unfurl its wings. This can take a bit of time, which is a problem when a predator is quickly approaching. Fortunately, the beetle's spray mechanism can be quickly deployed, giving the beetle the time it needs to set up and make its getaway.

| HABITAT | Woodlands or grasslands in temperate zones |
| RANGE | North America |

FIREFLY

FAMILY LAMPYRIDAE

Fireflies are beetles, not flies. Like stars twinkling on a summer night, fireflies catch our attention and imagination. More important, they draw the attention of their potential mates with their flashing signals. There are some 2,000 species in the firefly family, each with its own blinking patterns. Some types gather together in large numbers and blink on and off in perfect unison!

How do they make light? Fireflies use special cells inside light organs in their abdomen. Oxygen combines with a chemical called luciferin in the cells. Together they produce an enzyme responsible for making light. The chemical reaction is known as bioluminescence.

Adult fireflies lay their eggs on the ground. Both larvae and pupae light up, but they don't blink like adults. The larvae might live a couple of years underground, but the adults die after a few weeks.

Scientists have transferred the "light" gene found in fireflies into other organisms, including mice, monkeys, cats, and tobacco plants.

FACTS

OTHER COMMON NAME	Lightning bug	**SCIENTIFIC NAME**	Family: Lampyridae
SIZE	Up to 1.0 inch (25 mm)	**WINGS**	Yes in most
FOOD	Adult: some feed on pollen and mites; others don't eat at all / Larva: small invertebrates		

In addition to rotting plant matter and dung, the Goliath beetle feeds on tree sap.

FACTS

COMMON NAME Goliath beetle

WINGS Yes (their forewings are hardened wing covers and their hind wings are for flying)

SCIENTIFIC NAME *Goliathus goliatus* / Family: Scarabaeidae

SIZE 2.0–4.3 inches (50–110 mm)

FOOD Adult: scavenges on rotting plant matter and animal dung / Larva: decomposing wood, small insects, and other high-protein food

GOLIATH BEETLE

FAMILY SCARABAEIDAE

The Goliath is one of the world's largest beetles. It's also the heaviest. This colossal insect can measure up to 4.3 inches (110 mm) long and weighs up to 2.1 ounces (60 g). A Goliath beetle larva weighs up to 3.5 ounces (100 g). That makes it as heavy as some cell phones!

How does the Goliath beetle get so big? As a larva, the beetle feeds on plenty of high-protein foods. It continues to feed as it develops.

When the larva finally stops growing, it burrows into the ground, where it enters its pupal stage. During this stage, its tissues break down and are reorganized into an adult form. Because of the Goliath beetle's large size, this can take several months. When the process is complete, an adult Goliath beetle emerges.

Goliath beetles are named after the biblical character Goliath. In this famous tale, Goliath is a menacing giant who stands more than 9 feet (2.7 m) tall.

HABITAT Equatorial forests and savannas

RANGE Equatorial region of Africa

SACRED SCARAB

FAMILY SCARABAEIDAE

Sacred scarab beetles have a gross habit.

They roll dung balls. That's not all—they eat them too!

The beetles also use the dung balls to house their eggs and feed their young. The female lays a single egg inside a specially sculpted dung ball, which she keeps in an underground chamber. Inside, the larvae will feed on the dung and grow.

The sacred scarab got its name because of its history. The ancient Egyptians likened their god of the sunrise to the beetles. They noted the similarity between how the scarab beetle rolled its dung ball to how the sun rolled across the sky each day.

These beetles do a huge service to the environment by eating and burying animal dung, which fertilizes and loosens the soil.

FACTS

COMMON NAME	Sacred scarab	
SCIENTIFIC NAME	*Scarabaeus sacer* / Family: Scarabaeidae	
SIZE	1.10–1.26 inches (28–32 mm)	
WINGS	Yes (their forewings are hardened wing covers and their hind wings are for flying)	
FOOD	Adult and Larva: animal dung	

Dried dung beetles are used for all kinds of health treatments in traditional Chinese medicine.

HABITAT In coastal dunes and marshes

RANGE Around the Mediterranean Sea

This close-up of a hide beetle shows that the insect is covered with tiny hairs, or setae. The hairs produce a distinct pattern on each insect. Scientists use these unique patterns to help identify hide beetles in the field.

FACTS

COMMON NAME	Hide beetle	**SCIENTIFIC NAME**	*Dermestes maculatus* / Family: Dermestidae
SIZE	0.22–0.4 inch (5.5–10 mm)	**WINGS**	Yes (their forewings are hardened wing covers and their hind wings are for flying)
FOOD	Adult and Larva: dead animals		

HIDE BEETLE

FAMILY DERMESTIDAE

Hide beetles, dark and hairy, are best known for their somewhat creepy diet.

They feed on dead animals—and that includes humans!

This ability of theirs makes hide beetles somewhat unique. Most insects would be unable to digest an animal's keratin—a protein that makes up skin, fingernails, and hair—because the substance is too tough. But hide beetles have special enzymes in their digestive tract that help break down the material.

The beetle's diet has made it a favorite among forensic scientists. When these crime-scene specialists see the bugs on or near a dead body, they know the victim has been dead for quite some time. That's because the bugs only show up late in the body's decomposition process.

Hide beetles are used by natural history museums. Scientists rely on them to eat away fur and skin from the bones of dead animals. This helps the scientists prepare the bones for museum exhibitions.

HABITAT	Many different habitats
RANGE	Worldwide (except Antarctica)

HEADLIGHT ELATER

FAMILY ELATERIDAE

Shortly after sunset, the large headlight elater beetle becomes active. It gets its name from the two bright light organs on the upper part of its thorax. The headlights, along with a band on the lower part of its body, glow in the dark. In fact, the lights can get so bright, people are known to hold a headlight elater like a flashlight to light the trail in front of them. These beetles don't blink quickly like fireflies do, but they can signal to potential mates by keeping the lights on for a long period of time and blinking occasionally. The eggs, larvae, and pupae also glow.

There are various species of headlight elaters. The species *Pyrophorus noctilucus* is the largest of them. Headlight elaters are a few of the 9,300 or so species of click beetles. Click beetles snap their bodies very forcefully, catapulting themselves into the air about a foot or so high, and they can flip over when they're on their backs. They mainly use their click mechanism to defend themselves from predators.

If you pick up a click beetle and put it on your hand, it will click and jump to escape.

FACTS

COMMON NAME	Headlight elater
WINGS	Yes (their forewings are hardened wing covers and their hind wings are for flying)
SCIENTIFIC NAME	*Pyrophorus noctilucus* / Family: Elateridae
SIZE	1.6–2.0 inches (40–50 mm)
FOOD	Adult: pollen, fermenting fruit, and small insects / Larva: plant matter and small invertebrates

HABITAT Forests

RANGE Northern half of South America, Panama, Mexico, southern Florida, and Hawaii

FACTS

OTHER COMMON NAME   Eastern milkweed longhorn

SCIENTIFIC NAME   *Tetraopes tetrophthalmus* / Family: Cerambycidae

SIZE   0.4–0.63 inch (10–16 mm)

WINGS   Yes (their forewings are hardened wing covers and their hind wings are for flying)

FOOD   Adult: foliage and flowers of milkweed / Larva: stems and roots of milkweed

RED MILKWEED BEETLE

FAMILY CERAMBYCIDAE

The best place to find the red milkweed beetle is . . . you guessed it—on milkweed plants. Milkweeds have toxins that most insects can't handle, but red milkweed beetles have adapted to feeding on these plants without being harmed. In fact, they use the toxins they take in for protection. Predators that munch on the beetle experience a nasty taste surprise—and learn to keep the critter off their lunch menu in the future!

The beetle's milkweed diet isn't its only interesting feature. Unlike most insects, it has four eyes. The base of each antenna is positioned in a way that divides each eye in two.

These beetles belong to a huge family with more than 20,000 species. They are commonly known as longhorn beetles, named for their extremely long antennae.

One species of longhorn beetle (*Cyrtophones verrucosus*) is an ant mimic from North America. It not only looks like an ant, it also behaves like one by waving its antennae and walking in a zigzag motion.

HABITAT	Wherever the host plant is present, especially open areas
RANGE	Eastern and central North America

GIANT CARRION BEETLE

FAMILY SILPHIDAE

This big scavenger is an environmental hero. It feeds on dead, decaying animals, and then buries the leftovers in the ground. This helps recycle the dead matter into the ecosystem. The giant carrion beetle not only eats carrion, but raises its young on it too. In fact, these beetles will fight over a carcass—the winning male and female get to bury it!

Unlike most insects, male and female burying beetles raise their larvae together. After the female lays between 1 and 30 eggs next to the carcass, both mom and dad feed and tend their young. The larvae eat for about a week, then become pupae in the soil.

Unfortunately, giant carrion beetles are endangered. They have been drastically decreasing in numbers, and they have disappeared from 90 percent of their historic range. The reason for the decline isn't clear, though some experts believe pesticides and habitat loss could be to blame.

> The giant carrion beetle has chemical receptors on its clublike antennae that smell dead animals from almost two miles (3.2 km) away.

FACTS

OTHER COMMON NAME American burying beetle

SCIENTIFIC NAME *Nicrophorus americanus* / Family: Silphidae

SIZE 1.0–1.8 inches (25–45 mm)

WINGS Yes (their forewings are hardened wing covers and their hind wings are for flying)

FOOD Adult and Larva: carrion

158

A giant carrion beetle prepares a dead dove for burial.

HABITAT	Wherever carcasses of birds and small mammals can be found
RANGE	Once widespread, now in only a few states and being reintroduced into others

FACTS

COMMON NAME	Blue fungus beetle	**SCIENTIFIC NAME**	*Gibbifer californicus* / Family: Erotylidae
SIZE	0.5–0.8 inch (12–20 mm)	**WINGS**	Yes (their forewings are hardened wing covers and their hind wings are for flying)
FOOD	Adult and Larva: wood-rotting fungi		

BLUE FUNGUS BEETLE

FAMILY EROTYLIDAE

Not all beetles feed on plants or animals. Some, like the blue fungus beetle, can't produce the enzymes needed to break down plant or animal tissues, so they feed on fungi because it does the job for them.

Fungi, such as mushrooms, are nature's decomposers. They break down and digest nonliving organic matter such as decaying trees and leaves, as well as dead animals. The fungi absorb nutrients from the matter they decompose. So when the blue fungus beetle eats the fungi, it gets the nutrients it needs to survive.

Mother beetles of this species also use the fungus as a shelter for their eggs. When the larvae emerge from their shells, they don't have to go far for food. They are immediately treated to a fungus meal.

The blue fungus beetle belongs to the family known as the "pleasing fungus beetles." Members of this family are often brightly colored. They may also have patterns such as dots, stripes, and zigzags.

HABITAT	Moist areas at higher elevations
RANGE	Southwestern North America and northern Mexico

DARKLING BEETLE

FAMILY TENEBRIONIDAE

There are approximately 20,000 species of darkling beetles in the world. "Darkling" refers to the dark-colored elytra, or hardened forewings, sported by many of these creatures.

The name also refers to the insect's nocturnal habits. The beetle is mainly active at night, when it forages for food such as insect larvae and decaying plant and animal matter.

Foraging at night gives the darkling beetle some protection from predators that would have no trouble spotting the critter in daylight. However, if a predator does manage to detect the beetle, the beetle will fight back. Many species of darklings, such as the pinacate beetle, blast predators with a smelly liquid similar to that of the bombardier beetle. (See page 145.)

FACTS

COMMON NAME	Darkling beetle	**SCIENTIFIC NAME**	Family: Tenebrionidae
SIZE	0.08–2.0 inches (2–50 mm)	**WINGS**	Yes (their forewings are hardened wing covers and their hind wings are for flying)
		FOOD	Adult and Larva: plant matter, some decomposing animal matter, fungi

The darkling beetle shown here—a member of the *Alphitobius* genus—is from Tanzania, Africa.

Some darkling beetle species live in deserts, where water isn't always available. To stay hydrated, they take in water from fog that condenses on their forewings. They position themselves so their heads face down and the condensed water rolls into their mouths.

HABITAT Dry and arid regions

RANGE Worldwide

163

The giraffe weevil's neck is jointed, allowing it to bend.

FACTS

COMMON NAME Giraffe weevil

SIZE Up to 1 inch (25 mm)

FOOD Adult and Larva: small tree leaves

SCIENTIFIC NAME *Trachelophorus giraffa* / Family: Attelabidae

WINGS Yes (their forewings are hardened wing covers and their hind wings are for flying)

GIRAFFE WEEVIL

FAMILY ATTELABIDAE

A weevil is a type of small beetle that's known for its noselike snout.

Weevils often use their snouts to bore holes into the plants, fruits, or nuts that they feed on. For some weevils, their snout isn't their only striking feature. The male giraffe weevil has a superlong neck that is longer than the insect's body.

Male giraffe weevils use their necks to fight each other for the right to mate with a female. It's not common for males to kill each other during the battle, but the fighting can get pretty fierce. You might say the competition is neck and neck.

Giraffe weevils are especially fond of the small trees in Madagascar that have been named after them. They're called giraffe weevil trees.

Some weevil species, like the chestnut weevil (*Curculio caratrypes*), don't just use their long snouts to feed. They also use them to drill holes into nuts and fruit, where they lay their eggs.

HABITAT Forests

RANGE Madagascar

WEEVILS GALLERY

Weevils are a type of beetle with some 60,000 known species. Many of them have an elongated head called a snout with mouthparts at the tip. They chew their way into the grains, fruits, and roots of plants. Some weevils do this to extract food or to carve out a home for their eggs. Most weevils start life on the plants that they eat, and some weevils are pests on crop plants.

Although some species, like the giraffe weevil, can be a whole inch long, most weevils are smaller, rarely exceeding a quarter of an inch (6 mm). A weevil's tiny size can make it an easy target for larger predators, like spiders and birds. When most weevils are threatened by a predator, they react by dropping to the ground and playing dead. Since many weevils are similar in color to soil, they go undetected.

Check out the six species on this page.

The color of this flashy blue weevil is the result of light reflecting off tiny scales that cover the insect's body.

This palmetto weevil is lifting its elytra and unfolding its hind wings in preparation for flight. Palmetto weevils are known to cause a lot of damage to palm trees.

Many weevils draw up their legs, fall over, and play dead when discovered by a predator.

This close-up of the fungus weevil shows the many light-sensitive cells that make up the insect's compound eyes.

The shape of a weevil's snout is adapted for boring holes into its host plant. Since different weevils have different host plants, their nose shapes vary.

A few weevil species, like this one from the Amazonian rain forest, have snouts that are longer than their bodies!

A female eastern dobsonfly covers her eggs with a clear fluid. When the fluid dries, it turns a white color that resembles large bird droppings. This helps camouflage the eggs from predators.

FACTS

OTHER COMMON NAME Dobsonfly

SCIENTIFIC NAME *Corydalus cornutus* / Family: Corydalidae

SIZE Up to 2 inches (50 mm), not including male's mandibles

WINGS Yes

FOOD Adult: does not eat / Larva: aquatic insects and small fish

EASTERN DOBSONFLY

FAMILY CORYDALIDAE

The male eastern dobsonfly has long curved mandibles, or jaws, that measure up to 1 inch (25 mm) long. That's about three times the length of its head! The mandibles look like they pack quite a bite, but they're actually harmless.

The male uses his mandibles during courtship and mating. He'll flaunt his jaws in front of a female to impress her, or he'll use them to wrestle other males. The victor of the match wins the right to mate with the female. The female lays her eggs on leaves overhanging a stream. The eggs hatch and the small larvae drop into the water.

The larvae develop gills and are called hellgrammites. They live, often for years, under rocks in streams, rivers, and lakes. The jaws of a dobsonfly larva are much smaller, but not as harmless as the adult's. These maturing dobsonflies use their sharp, forward-pointing mandibles to inflict a painful bite on any predator that threatens them. Ouch!

When the time is right, the large larvae crawl out of the water and dig underground chambers, where they make silk cocoons before becoming pupae.

The adult male dobsonfly's pincers look threatening, but they're only used during mating. Females, on the other hand, use their shorter pincers to bite.

HABITAT	Near rivers and streams
RANGE	Eastern parts of North America

ANTLION

FAMILY MYRMELEONTIDAE

Antlion larvae, sometimes called doodlebugs, are cunning predators with huge sickle-shaped jaws. In some species, the larva creates a pitfall trap to capture prey. It digs a sand pit and buries itself in the middle, just under the surface. Its wide-open jaws face upward to catch insects, especially ants that stumble into the sand trap. There are more than 1,500 species of antlions worldwide; they are especially common in semi-arid areas.

All adult antlion species look a little like damselflies (see pp. 68–69) but with thicker, clubbed antennae. Females lay their eggs in the sand or dust. When a larva matures, it makes a silk and sand cocoon underground and then transforms into a pupa. When the adult emerges, it climbs to the surface and flies in search of a mate.

FACTS

OTHER COMMON NAME	Doodlebug	**SCIENTIFIC NAME**	Family: Myrmeleontidae
SIZE	1.75 inch (45 mm)	**WINGS**	Yes
FOOD	Adult: occasionally eats nectar, pollen, and insects / Larva: ants and other small insects		

In the United States, antlions are often called doodlebugs because their larvae make doodle-like impressions in the surface of the sand as they search for a new place to make a sand pit.

HABITAT Dry locations with fine sand or dust

RANGE Worldwide

171

Lacewing larvae feed on various soft-bodied insects, especially aphids. For that reason, they're sometimes called "aphid lions." A larva measures only 0.5 inches (12 mm), but can eat about 200 aphids in just one week!

FACTS

COMMON NAME Common green lacewing

SCIENTIFIC NAME Family: Chrysopidae

SIZE 0.6–0.8 inch (15–20 mm)

WINGS Yes

FOOD Adult: pollen, nectar, honeydew / Larva: insects, including aphids, leafhoppers, moths, and caterpillars

COMMON GREEN LACEWING

FAMILY CHRYSOPIDAE

Like lace bugs (see pp. 126–127), the green lacewing has netlike patterns on its wings that resemble lace. The green lacewing's wings aren't just pretty; they serve an important function by helping the insect avoid bats.

Bats are major predators of the green lacewings. When these winged mammals are on the hunt, they emit sound waves that travel through the air. When the waves hit an object—like a lacewing—they bounce back to the bat. This tells the bat where the object (in this case, its prey) is located. Fortunately, the green lacewing has special organs at the base of its forewings that pick up vibrations, including those emitted by bats. These vibrations usually give the lacewing enough time to dodge the flying mammal.

HABITAT Open fields with plenty of vegetation

RANGE United States, Europe, Asia

173

TARANTULA HAWK

FAMILY POMPILIDAE

Tarantula hawks are huge wasps that can deliver a walloping sting. Most predatory animals won't touch them.

To reproduce, the female tarantula hawk finds and stings tarantulas, and then drags them, sometimes over long distances, to her burrow or a specially prepared nest. She lays a single egg on the abdomen of a paralyzed tarantula, and then buries it alive. After hatching, the wasp larva eats the inside of the spider. At first, it avoids the spider's vital organs. This delays the spider's death, and thus gives the wasp time to develop.

Male tarantula hawks search for mates by hill-topping. They sit on tall plants on hills and watch for passing females that are ready to mate.

One easy way to tell tarantula hawk males and females apart is to look at their antennae. The male's antennae are straight and the female's are coiled near the tips. Only the female tarantula hawk has a stinger. It's the same organ (ovipositor) that she uses to lay eggs.

FACTS

COMMON NAME	Tarantula hawk
SCIENTIFIC NAME	*Pepsis* and *Hemipepsis* / Family: Pompilidae
SIZE	About 0.5–2.75 inches (12–69.9 mm) in length (for the genus *Pepsis*)
WINGS	Yes
FOOD	Adult: nectar / Larva: tarantulas

HABITAT Where tarantulas are found, from rain forests to deserts

RANGE India, Southeast Asia, Australia, Europe, Africa, the Americas

This paper wasp works on building the cells of its nest. Some paper wasp nests contain 200 cells.

FACTS

OTHER COMMON NAME Umbrella wasp

SCIENTIFIC NAME Subfamily: Polistinae / Family: Vespidae

SIZE Under 0.7–1.0 inch (18–25 mm)

WINGS Yes

FOOD Adult: nectar and honeydew / Larva: insects such as caterpillars

PAPER WASP

FAMILY VESPIDAE

Paper wasps are the builders of the insect world, with a real knack for nest construction. To build their nests, most paper wasp species begin by gathering fibers from dead wood and plants. They mix the materials together with their saliva, and then shape the mixture into clusters of comb-shaped cells. When the nest cells dry, they have a paperlike quality. The nests are also water-repellant, which keeps them dry in the rain. The wasps build their nests in sheltered areas, including tree branches and the eaves of houses. For added protection, the wasps secrete a chemical around their nest. The chemical repels ants that would otherwise feed on the eggs stored inside the nest.

Scientists have discovered that one paper wasp species, *Polistes fuscatus*, can recognize individuals of its type by the patterns on their faces. Their ability to recognize faces is much like our own ability to do so!

HABITAT	Urban areas, meadows, and grasslands
RANGE	Worldwide

EASTERN YELLOW JACKET

FAMILY VESPIDAE

Eastern yellow jacket adults prefer to eat sugary treats such as nectar, but when it comes to feeding their young, only meat will do.

After their larvae hatch from the eggs, the adult seeks out an insect, such as a caterpillar, or a nice, juicy spider. The yellow jacket uses its legs to grab its prey and stings the spider if it puts up a fight. Once the spider is firmly in its grip, the yellow jacket rips off the spider's cephalothorax (head-thorax) and legs. Then, it sinks its mouthparts into what's left of the spider's body to suck out its insides.

Next, the yellow jacket drags the spider's remains to the nest. There, it vomits the contents of its digested meal for the newly hatched larvae to feed on. After a few days, when the larvae are older, they feed on solid pieces of the spider's body.

FACTS

COMMON NAME	Eastern yellow jacket
SCIENTIFIC NAME	*Vespula maculifrons* / Family: Vespidae
SIZE	Up to 0.75 inch (19 mm)
FOOD	Adult: sugary foods such as nectar / Larva: spiders and insects
WINGS	Yes

This Eastern yellow jacket feeds on the nectar of goldenrod flowers and is covered with pollen.

Some yellow jacket nests can be huge. In 2006, a man in Tallassee, Alabama, discovered a yellow jacket nest that was so large it filled his entire car!

HABITAT Cities, suburbs, and farmland

RANGE Eastern North America, as well as the Great Plains of the United States

Almost all 60,000 or so named species of Ichneumon wasps are parasitoids. They feed on the larvae and pupae of other insects like butterflies, moths, beetles, bees, and aphids. Some even deposit their eggs inside spiders. When the wasp's larvae hatch from the eggs, they eat the spider!

The female irritator wasp uses her long ovipositor to drill a hole in wood.

FACTS

COMMON NAME	Irritator wasp
SCIENTIFIC NAME	*Dolichomitus irritator* / Family: Ichneumonidae
SIZE	About 0.875 inches (22 mm), without ovipositor
WINGS	Yes
FOOD	Adult: nectar / Larva: wood-boring beetles and weevils

~~IRRITATOR~~ WASP

FAMILY ICHNEUMONIDAE

Like most other solitary wasps in the family Ichneumonidae, the irritator wasp has a superlong ovipositor, a thin tube that extends from its rear. The ovipositor can measure up to 1.5 inches (3.8 cm), making it as long as the insect's head and body combined. In general, wasps use their ovipositor to lay eggs. But it has another important function for this species.

The irritator wasp uses its ovipositor to drill holes into the wood of trees. This helps the insect gain access to any beetles nestled inside the wood.

When the irritator wasp reaches the beetle, it deposits its eggs on the insect. If the beetle tries to escape, the wasp will inject it with a toxin to temporarily paralyze it. When larvae ultimately emerge from the eggs, they feed on the beetle.

As the female at left deposits her eggs, a pouch at the tip of her abdomen keeps her ovipositor steady.

HABITAT Woodland and brush

RANGE North America

OAK APPLE GALL WASP

FAMILY CYNIPIDAE

Like many insects, female gall wasps lay their eggs on plant leaves. But after the eggs hatch, something strange happens. The larvae trigger a chemical reaction in the plant. The plant tissues begin to grow and form a protective covering over the newly hatched larvae. The covering is called a gall.

Galls can vary in shape and size, depending on the species they house. A gall produced by an oak apple gall wasp is about 2 inches (5 cm) wide and is shaped like an apple. The gall provides the wasp larva with nutrients as it develops inside. When the wasp becomes an adult, it bores a hole through the gall and emerges.

Wasps have a narrow junction between their thorax and abdomen, which gives them the appearance of having a narrow waist. This "wasp waist" was the inspiration for a once-popular fashion concept that began in the 1800s: Women used supertight corsets to draw in their waists.

FACTS

COMMON NAME	Oak apple gall wasp
SIZE	Under 0.25 inch (6 mm)
SCIENTIFIC NAME	*Amphibolips confluenta* / Family: Cynipidae
WINGS	Yes
FOOD	Adult and Larva: black oak and southern red oak

This gall, which looks like an apple, contains a developing larva.

HABITAT	Wherever black and southern red oaks are found
RANGE	North America

When velvet ants are threatened, they make a squeaking sound by rubbing two parts of their body together. Females can also deliver a sting that's lethal to some insects. The sting is so painful that the wasps are sometimes called "cow killers." However, there is no evidence of a velvet ant ever killing a cow!

FACTS

OTHER COMMON NAME Eastern velvet ant

SCIENTIFIC NAME *Dasymutilla occidentalis* / Family: Mutillidae

SIZE Up to 0.75 inch (19 mm)

WINGS Present only in males

FOOD Adult: nectar / Larva: larvae of other insects

RED VELVET ANT

FAMILY MUTILLIDAE

Red velvet ants aren't really ants. They're actually wasps, but the female members of the group have wingless, ant-shaped bodies. Males, on the other hand, have wings.

Both females and males are covered with dense velvety bristles that give them a soft appearance. However, the opposite is actually true. Red velvet ants have a very tough exoskeleton. This trait prevents them from losing moisture in the dry areas that they inhabit. It also helps protect them from the stings of bumblebees and other wasps.

Why would bumblebees and other wasps attack the velvet ants? Female velvet ants have been known to crawl into these insects' nests and deposit their eggs there. So when larvae hatch from the eggs, they have instant access to their prey.

HABITAT	Meadows, fields, edge of forests
RANGE	Eastern states south of New England and Gulf states in the U.S.

185

WASPS GALLERY

Scientists divide wasps into two main groups: social and solitary. Social wasps live together in colonies that consist of a queen, workers, and drones. The drones and queen mate to produce young. The queen is responsible for nest construction, which she continues to work on until she is ready to lay her eggs. At that point, the workers take over the nest-building duties. The workers also feed the young larvae after they have hatched from the eggs.

Unlike social wasps, solitary wasps live alone. In addition, the queen lays her eggs on or beside a host—usually an insect or spider. When the parasitoid larvae hatch from the eggs, they feed on their host.

There are 30,000 species of wasps in the world. Depending on the species, they can range in color from dull brown or black to bright blue or red. To get a sense of just how varied wasps are, check out the critters shown here.

After stinging a katydid, a sand wasp hauls the insect to its sandy burrow, where the wasp's larvae will feed on it.

These paper wasps work on constructing the hexagon-shaped cells of their nest. Eventually, each cell will house one egg.

The potter wasp zips back to its nest with a tasty caterpillar. The wasp itself won't eat the caterpillar. Instead, it will leave it for one of its developing larvae to eat.

This paper nest, created by vespid wasps, is anchored to a tree branch. A large entrance can be seen at the bottom, and smaller ones are higher up.

This wasp is chomping on the wood of a gatepost. It will chew the wood into a pasty pulp, which it will use to build its nest.

This insect is one of two red wasp species in the eastern part of North America.

187

WESTERN HONEYBEE

FAMILY APIDAE

A colony of honeybees live together in a hive, where they have many responsibilities that range from collecting nectar and pollen to hive construction. Most of the work is done by the colony's female worker bees.

The worker bees travel from flower to flower in search of pollen and nectar. The pollen gets stuck on the bee's body hairs. Then the bee brushes the pollen into structures on its hind legs, called pollen baskets, and stores the nectar in a special pouch. Back at the hive, the pollen and nectar are processed by another group of worker bees to make honey.

The workers are also in charge of building the hive's cells, or rooms. They build these six-sided cells from a waxy substance secreted from their bodies. The cells are used to store honey and to house developing larvae and pupae.

In addition, the workers tend to the queen bee, which mates with males called drones to produce the eggs. The workers feed the queen bee "royal jelly," a mixture that includes proteins, sugar, and fatty acids. They also provide food for her larvae.

The western honeybee stores pollen inside small cavities in its hind legs. These cavities are known as pollen baskets.

FACTS

OTHER COMMON NAME	European honeybee
SCIENTIFIC NAME	*Apis mellifera* / Family: Apidae
SIZE	0.4–0.7 inch (10–18 mm); queens: 0.7–0.8 inch (18–20 mm)
WINGS	Yes
FOOD	Adult: pollen, nectar, honey, and in some cases, secretions called royal jelly / Larva: royal jelly and bee bread

When a worker honeybee locates a food source, she returns to the hive to share the news. If the food is located up to 80 feet (25 m) away, she does a round dance. If the food is 80–330 feet (25–100 m) away, she does a waggle dance. The direction in which the honeybee moves while performing the waggle dance tells the other bees where to go to find the food source.

In the wild, up to 20,000 honeybees can live in a hive!

HABITAT Areas with flowering plants, such as meadows and gardens

RANGE Worldwide

189

Unlike other male bee species, which have yellow facial hair, the male buff-tailed bumblebee has black hair on its face.

FACTS

OTHER COMMON NAMES	Large earth bumblebee, humble-bee		**SCIENTIFIC NAME**	*Bombus terrestris* / Family: Apidae
SIZE	0.6–1.0 inch (15–25 mm)	**WINGS** Yes	**FOOD**	Adult and Larva: pollen and nectar

BUFF-TAILED BUMBLEBEE

FAMILY APIDAE

Like honeybees, the buff-tailed bumblebees travel among flowers collecting nectar—and sometimes pollen—to produce honey (photo at right). But the bumblebee species differs from its honeybee cousin in many ways. Unlike honeybees, which live in hives aboveground, buff-tailed bumblebee colonies reside in underground nests. Often, the nests are housed in former mouse burrows.

Also, while the honeybee stays active year-round, most buff-tailed bumblebees can survive only during warmer months. Why? The bees need to heat their bodies in order to fly. They can generate some heat by shivering, but rely mainly on the sun's warm rays to do the job. This becomes difficult when temperatures dip in late fall and early winter. When the bumblebee is unable to fly, it can't collect food, and therefore starves.

The buff-tailed bumblebee queen is usually one of only a few colony members to survive the winter. In the spring, she begins a new colony.

Bumblebees are not aggressive and so are not likely to sting, except very close to their nest. Only the queen and worker bees can sting, not the males. A bumblebee's stinger is smooth, and the bee can sting more than once, unlike a honeybee, which has a barbed stinger and stings only once, then dies.

HABITAT Edge of forests, in meadows and grasslands

RANGE Europe, North Africa, parts of Asia, New Zealand

NEON CUCKOO BEE

FAMILY APIDAE

Cuckoo birds have a bad reputation for laying their eggs in the nests of other birds—and the cuckoo bee is no different.

The neon cuckoo bee sneaks into the nest of the blue-banded bee, usually while its hosts are out collecting nectar and pollen for their own colony. The cuckoo bee then lays its eggs, as well as a food supply, inside the cells that house the colony's own eggs. When the cuckoo larvae hatch, they attack and kill the blue-banded bee colony's larvae and then feed on the food inside the cells.

Sometimes, the blue-banded bees are actually present when the cuckoo bee sneaks in. Since the bees are similar in color, the invader can go undetected by the colony.

> To gain control of the host nest, some cuckoo bee species will kill the queen. They then use physical attacks or their pheromones (chemicals that influence behavior) to control the nest's workers.

FACTS

COMMON NAME	Neon cuckoo bee	**SCIENTIFIC NAME**	*Thyreus nitidulus* / Family: Apidae
SIZE	0.4–0.6 inch (10–14 mm)	**WINGS**	Yes
FOOD	Adult: pollen and nectar / Larva: larvae of other bees, pollen, and nectar		

HABITAT Woodlands and urban areas

RANGE Throughout most of Australia

This bulldog ant leans over to take a sip of water.

FACTS

COMMON NAME   Bulldog ant

SCIENTIFIC NAME   *Myrmecia* / Family: Formicidae

SIZE   Can grow to more than 1.6 inches (40 mm)

WINGS   Present in some species

FOOD   Adult: small insects, honeydew, seeds, fungi / Larva: dead insects

BULLDOG ANT

FAMILY FORMICIDAE

Australia's bulldog ants are some of the largest ants in the world. An adult bulldog ant can measure more than one inch (25 mm) long.

Bulldog ants are as ferocious as they are big. They have sharp serrated jaws and a powerful sting, which they'll use against anything that gets in their way. But their main target is their prey.

Bulldog ants are typically ambush hunters. They remain hidden, sometimes under a leaf, until they see their prey walk by. At that instant, the ant leaps onto its victim's back and stabs it with its stinger. Ouch!

The bulldog ant then feeds on the animal's juices and drags the carcass back to its nest. There, ant larvae consume the remains.

Bulldog ants have amazing jumping abilities. The ants are known to pounce on flying insects, such as wasps!

HABITAT	Urban areas, forests, woodland, heath
RANGE	Australia and New Caledonia

WEAVER ANT

FAMILY FORMICIDAE

Weaver ant colonies live in leafy nests located in the trees of Africa, Australia, and Asia. To build these nests, the ants rely on the colony's larvae.

Weaver ant larvae secrete a sticky silk-like substance from their heads. Adults use this substance like glue. While a few worker ants hold together two leaves, a third worker gently holds a larva with its mandibles (photo above). The worker then taps the larva on the head with its antenna, signaling for it to produce the "glue." When the larva secretes the substance, the workers use it to seal the leaves together. The workers and larvae continue this process until they have built a nest.

Weaver ant nests aren't just populated by weaver ants. The caterpillar of a certain butterfly species (*Liphyra brassolis*) might also reside in the nest. The thick-skinned caterpillar feeds on the ants' eggs and larvae. Often, the ants fight back, but they are unable to defeat their unwelcome houseguests.

FACTS

COMMON NAME	Weaver ant	**SCIENTIFIC NAME**	*Oecophylla smaragdina* / Family: Formicidae
SIZE	0.3–0.4 inch (8–10 mm)	**WINGS**	Queen has wings, which she sheds
FOOD	Adult: mainly nectar and honeydew / Larva: secretions from the queen ant and regurgitated food		

Weaver ants stiffen their bodies and rear up on their hind legs to show aggression.

HABITAT Forested areas

RANGE Australia, Asia, parts of Africa

197

The smallest worker ants, called "minima," are responsible for feeding the larger workers and protecting them from parasites. They often hitch a ride on the leaves that other members carry. The largest worker ants, called "majors," aggressively protect the colony with their huge, sharp mandibles (see p. 41).

FACTS

COMMON NAME	Leafcutter ant	**SCIENTIFIC NAME**	*Atta* / Family: Formicidae
SIZE	Workers are 0.08–0.6 inch (2–15 mm); queen is 0.9 inch (22 mm); males are 0.7 inch (18 mm)	**WINGS**	Yes
FOOD	Adult: fungus / Larva: regurgitated food		

LEAFCUTTER ANT

FAMILY FORMICIDAE

Leafcutter ants are the gardeners of the insect world. However, these social insects don't help plants to grow. Instead, they grow a type of fungus, which they eat. How do they do it?

First, worker ants find leaves that will help their fungus garden grow. As they travel in a line through the forest, they leave behind a scent trail. The scent helps them find their way back home.

When the ants come upon a group of leafy plants, they get to work. They use their mandibles, or jaws, to cut the leaves, flowers, and stems into pieces, and then carry them back to their nest.

In the nest, a different group of workers chew the leaves and plant parts into a pulp and deposit it onto the fungus garden. The pulp helps the fungus grow, so the ants will have plenty to eat.

The leafcutter ants are very protective of their food supply. When they detect any disease-causing microorganisms on the fungus, the ants remove the infested fungus, along with other waste, and place them in a special waste chamber or in a heap outside the nest.

This leafcutter ant uses its mandibles to cut off a piece of leaf.

HABITAT	Rain forest floor
RANGE	Central and South America

DOG AND CAT FLEA

FAMILY PULICIDAE

Does your dog or cat have an itch he just can't scratch? If so, he may have fleas. As these tiny parasites feed on your pet's blood, they produce saliva that can irritate the dog or cat's skin. And it seems like no amount of scratching can get rid of the flea. Why?

One reason is the flea's cling-on ability. The flea's joints are covered with spines. The spines work like a comb or the bristles of a brush to help the flea cling onto fur, even when the dog or cat makes sudden movements.

In addition, the flea has amazing jumping abilities—thanks largely to its pleural arch, a structure in its hind legs made of elastic protein. The arch is usually compressed, but when the flea's hind muscles relax, it is released. This allows the flea to take a high-flying leap—and dodge your pet's scratching leg.

Fleas are able to jump horizontally up to 13 inches (33 cm) and vertically up to 7 inches (17.7 cm). In the insect world, only the froghopper can reach a greater height with one leap.

FACTS

COMMON NAMES	Dog flea, cat flea
SCIENTIFIC NAME	*Ctenocephalides canis* and *C. felis* / Family: Pulicidae
SIZE	0.06–0.08 inch (1.5–2.0 mm)
WINGS	No
FOOD	Adult: blood of dogs, cats, and, sometimes, humans / Larva: adult flea feces, as well as dead skin and food particles

This photo shows what a cat flea looks like under a scanning electron microscope. Studies show that young cats have more fleas than older ones— most likely because they have poorer grooming habits.

HABITAT In dog and cat fur

RANGE Worldwide

FACTS

COMMON NAME Mosquito

SCIENTIFIC NAME Family: Culicidae

SIZE 0.125–0.75 inch (3–20 mm)

WINGS Front wings for flying and hind wings (called halteres) for balancing

FOOD Adult: nectar, honeydew, water, and the female takes blood meals / Larva: algae, bacteria, various microbes

MOSQUITO

FAMILY CULICIDAE

In most of the 3,500-plus species found worldwide, the female mosquito is a bloodthirsty pest.

She requires an occasional blood meal in order to get enough nutrients to make her eggs.

The mosquito uses her keen sense of smell to search for warm-blooded vertebrates, including people. She is able to detect exhaled carbon dioxide and chemicals in a person's sweat. When the female mosquito takes a blood meal, she injects saliva in order to prevent the blood from clogging her proboscis. The proboscis is like a syringe—long and hollow.

Mosquitoes are mostly active at dawn and dusk. People need to be especially cautious at those times. In certain places, unfortunately, mosquitoes carry infectious diseases and parasites that they transfer to human hosts—diseases such as malaria, yellow fever, dengue fever, and West Nile virus. Over one million people die each year from mosquito-borne diseases.

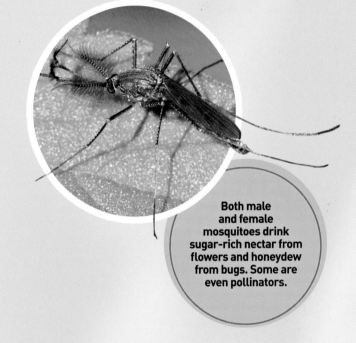

Both male and female mosquitoes drink sugar-rich nectar from flowers and honeydew from bugs. Some are even pollinators.

HABITAT Moist soils, standing water (tree holes, woodland pools, and swamps)

RANGE Worldwide

MARSH CRANE FLY

FAMILY TIPULIDAE

It's easy to confuse the marsh crane fly for a giant mosquito. Crane flies have long, spindly legs and thin abdomens like a mosquito. But they are different. Unlike mosquitoes, the crane fly is a poor flyer and wobbles in flight, and these flies don't bite people. However, young crane flies are destructive to our food supply. They eat the roots of cereal crops, potatoes, cabbage, raspberries, strawberries, onions, garlic, clover, and grasses. In contrast, many adults don't feed at all!

The marsh crane fly also differs from mosquitoes in its egg-laying methods. Most mosquitoes deposit their eggs on the water's surface, but the crane fly prefers soil. To lay eggs, the female aims her pointy abdomen straight down and hops along the soil, laying an egg each time she lands. When the larvae hatch from their eggs, they go to work eating the roots of young plants.

The front wings of this crane fly lie closed over its back. Looking like little knobs on a thread, the hind wings work to help balance the insect in flight.

FACTS

COMMON NAME	Marsh crane fly
SCIENTIFIC NAME	*Tipula oleracea* / Family: Tipulidae
SIZE	Body length up to 1.02 inches (26 mm)
WINGS	Front wings for flying and hind wings (called halteres) for balancing
FOOD	Adult: doesn't eat / Larva: grass roots, cereal crops, potatoes, cabbage, raspberries, strawberries, clover, onions, and garlic

One word or two? You'll see common names like crane fly and fruit fly in which "fly" is a separate word. You'll also see combined names like "mayfly," "dragonfly," "caddisfly," and "dobsonfly." If fly is a separate word, it belongs to the order Diptera ("true flies"). Otherwise it belongs to a different order.

HABITAT Gardens, pastures, meadows, moist places

RANGE North America, Canada, Europe, Asia, Arabia, North Africa, and Ecuador

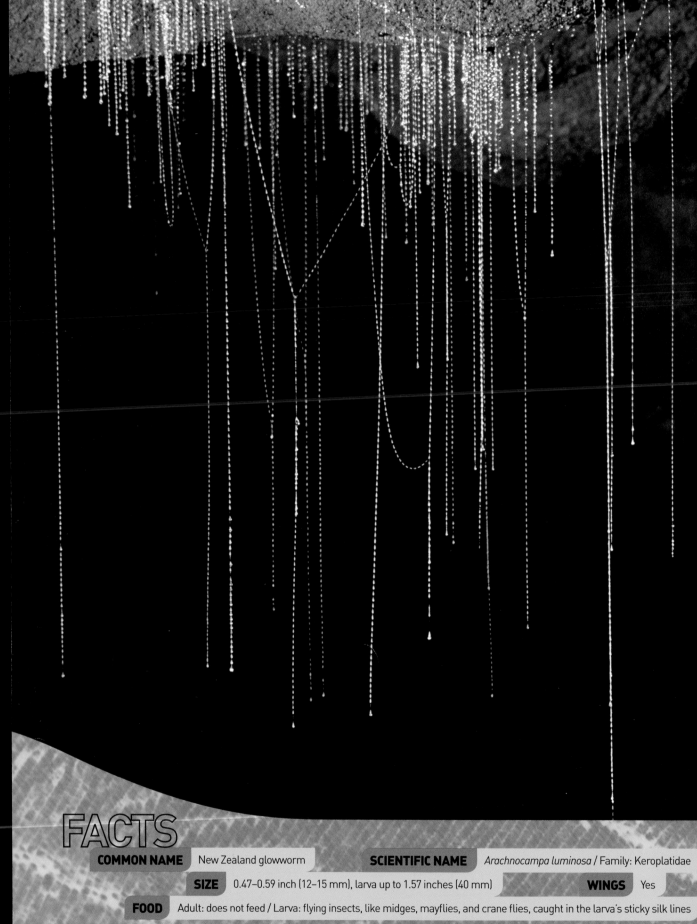

NEW ZEALAND GLOWWORM

FAMILY KEROPLATIDAE

The larvae of the New Zealand glowworm live on the ceilings of caves and other damp, dark places. They make silk "fishing lines" dotted with tiny blobs of glue to trap flying insects, their food. The best part is they glow in the dark—much the same way as firefly larvae. However, this glowworm is a fly, not a beetle like the firefly. Its glow is so bright that it lights up the dangling sticky lines.

The New Zealand glowworms attract more than prey with their light. They are a major tourist attraction too. One of the best known places to see them is the Glowworm Cave at Waitomo on the North Island of New Zealand.

Their scientific name means "glowing spider-worm," because they hunt with silk, like spiders do.

When the larvae become pupae, they still glow part of the time. When a female pupa is about to turn into an adult, her glow increases—and that attracts potential mates. But the males must wait around until she transforms into an adult.

HABITAT	Caves, grottoes, and damp, dark, protected places in the forest
RANGE	New Zealand

MEDITERRANEAN FRUIT FLY

FAMILY TEPHRITIDAE

As with all fruit flies, the larvae of a Mediterranean fruit fly (nicknamed "medfly") develop in moist places where there is water and organic matter that is rich in nutrients from dead organisms.

The female members of the family have a sharp ovipositor, which they use to pierce the skin of fruit and lay their eggs inside. Species like the medfly aren't too picky about the fruit they select. It can include apricots, avocados, grapefruit, and tomatoes. This has caused problems for farmers in the medfly's native region of East Africa, and eventually all over the world.

According to experts, fruits containing medfly larvae ship to other countries. After the larvae hatch from their eggs, they invade the crops of their new homes, becoming invasive species.

Today, the medfly is a huge problem in Hawaii, where it has destroyed a variety of crops, including papaya and guava.

A medfly maggot (larva) feeds on the inside of a piece of fruit. Its head, which appears at the bottom of this photo, has a mouth with hooklike teeth.

FACTS

OTHER COMMON NAME	Medfly
SCIENTIFIC NAME	*Ceratitis capitata* / Family: Tephritidae
SIZE	0.12–0.20 inch (3–5 mm)
WINGS	Yes
FOOD	Adult: juices of ripe and decomposing fruits, and bird feces / Larva: fruits and some vegetables

Another fruit fly
(*Zonosemata vittigera*)
from the same family
imitates a jumping spider to
protect itself from being eaten by
the spiders. The fly has what looks
like a spider leg pattern on its wings,
which it waves to mimic a jumping
spider's combative dance. When
the spider sees the fly displaying,
it displays in turn, and
then retreats.

HABITAT Wide-ranging, including forests, open woodland, and coasts

RANGE Worldwide

These female biting midges are feeding on a human hand.

FACTS

OTHER COMMON NAME No-see-um

SCIENTIFIC NAME *Leptoconops* / Family: Ceratopogonidae

SIZE 0.04–0.10 inch (1–3 mm)

WINGS Yes (front wings for flying and hind wings, called halteres, for balancing)

FOOD Adult: blood (females only) and nectar / Larva: small organisms; some species feed on bacteria, fungi, and algae

BITING MIDGE

FAMILY CERATOPOGONIDAE

Biting midges are tiny insects, measuring only 0.04 to 0.10 inch (1 to 3 mm) long.

Their tiny size is the reason why they are sometimes called "no-see-ums."

Like mosquitoes, female midges need to feed on blood in order to get enough protein in their diet to produce their eggs. To get blood, they'll bite any organism they come across. That includes other insects and mammals—and humans, too.

Unlike mosquitoes, biting midges don't pierce the skin. Instead, they use their scissorlike mouthparts to cut it open. After the cut is made, the midge injects an anticlotting chemical into the blood to ensure it flows freely. At that point, the midge is ready to suck.

The more blood a female biting midge consumes, the more eggs she will produce. One species, *Culicoides furens,* can lay up to 110 eggs after a blood meal.

HABITAT	Common in salt marshes and tropical areas, and in rotting fruit
RANGE	Tropical and subtropical areas, Caribbean, coastal areas of Florida

FLESH FLY

FAMILY SARCOPHAGIDAE

Flesh flies belong to a family of insects called Sarcophagidae. The name, which is made up of the Greek words for "flesh" and "eating," refers to the fly's tendency to feed on dead animals (called carrion). This includes insects, snails, and amphibians, such as frogs and toads.

The flesh fly also uses the carrion as a host for its developing larvae. The female produces eggs inside her body. After they hatch, she deposits them into the body of the animal, where they mature. The host animal is usually dead, but there are a few exceptions. One species, *Sarcophaga kellyi*, deposits its larvae onto a live grasshopper. The little maggots then burrow into the insect and feed on its organs. They remain inside the grasshopper until they are ready to enter the pupal stage. At that point, they make their exit and drop into the soil.

The Eastern flesh fly *(Sarcophaga sarraceniae)* deposits her larvae into a pitcher plant—a plant that kills and eats insects. The larvae feed on the dead insects inside the plant.

FACTS

COMMON NAME	Flesh fly	**SCIENTIFIC NAME**	Family: Sarcophagidae
SIZE	0.4–0.9 inch (10–22 mm)	**WINGS**	Yes (front wings for flying and hind wings, called halteres, for balancing)
FOOD	Adult and Larva: dead and decaying organisms; one species feeds on living grasshoppers		

The flesh fly can be distinguished from the common house fly by the stripes on its thorax. The flesh fly has three dark stripes while the house fly has four.

HABITAT Wide-ranging rural and urban areas

RANGE Worldwide

213

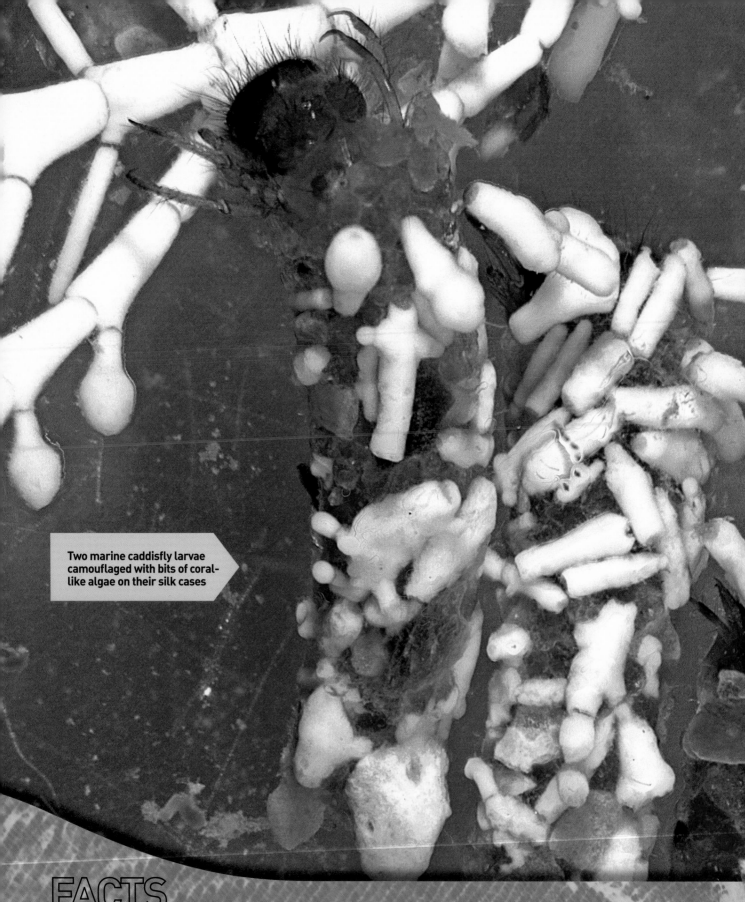

Two marine caddisfly larvae camouflaged with bits of coral-like algae on their silk cases

FACTS

OTHER COMMON NAME Sedge fly

SIZE 0.06–1.57 inches (1.5–40 mm)

SCIENTIFIC NAME Order: Trichoptera

FOOD Adult: most do not feed / Larva: small insects, leaves, algae

WINGS Yes

CADDISFLY

ORDER TRICHOPTERA

Caddisflies make up an order of insects with about 12,000 species. They are closely related to butterflies and moths, having two pairs of thin wings. But unlike those of butterflies and moths, their wings are hairy instead of scaly. Most larvae live in fresh water, but a few species are marine, meaning they live in the sea. One remarkable species from New Zealand and southern Australia *(Philanisus plebeius)* starts its life inside a cushion star (a type of sea star). How did it get there? The mother caddisfly has a long ovipositor for laying her eggs. During low tide, she flies up and down the coastline, and, when sea stars are exposed to the air, lays her eggs inside them.

After about one month, the larva hatches and makes its way out of the sea star. It then lives in tide pools, feeding on red algae. It makes a tubelike silk case to surround its body, which it often camouflages with bits of algae. It pokes its head out of its case to feed and move. After several larval molts, it turns into a pupa on the red algae. Eventually, an adult will emerge and fly free.

Most caddisfly larvae build a protective case around themselves by secreting a sticky silk and then decorating it with materials such as sand, gravel, and debris. Some people take advantage of the caddisfly's natural ability by having captive larvae construct jewelry from gemstones and bits of precious metals.

A freshwater caddisfly pupa in its case, which is camouflaged with stones

HABITAT	Near streams, ponds, and other bodies of water. Larvae live in water.
RANGE	All continents except Antarctica

MORPHO

FAMILY NYMPHALIDAE

There's nothing like seeing a huge metallic-blue butterfly dancing across the rain forest canopy. You can find about 80 morpho species in the tropical areas of Central and South America and Mexico. Many of them have iridescent blue on the top side of their wings. This may help other morphos to identify their own kind. But when a morpho comes to rest on the forest floor, it seems to disappear. That's because it closes its wings so only the lower sides of them are visible. The lower side is camouflaged with a mottled brown coloration. Morphos also have eyespots on their wings that may deceive predators such as insect-eating birds, lizards, and frogs.

Males form territories and patrol along streams and rivers during the late morning. They chase away rivals. In many species, only the male is brightly colored. The female is duller.

FACTS

COMMON NAME	Morpho	
SCIENTIFIC NAME	*Morpho* / Family: Nymphalidae	
SIZE	Wingspan from 3–8 inches (76–200 mm)	**WINGS** Yes
FOOD	Adult: rotting fruit on the forest floor sap / Larva: grasses, legumes, and other plants depending on species	

Morphos don't drink nectar from flowers, but feed on juices from rotting fruit and on sap flowing from wounds on trees and vines.

HABITAT Primary rain forest and other woodlands

RANGE Tropical Central and South America and Mexico

Several other butterfly species mimic the monarch's bright orange and black coloration, including viceroys, queens, and soldiers.

FACTS

COMMON NAME	Monarch	**SCIENTIFIC NAME**	*Danaus plexippus* / Family: Nymphalidae
SIZE	Wingspan: 3.5–4.0 inches (89–102 mm)	**WINGS**	Yes
FOOD	Adult: nectar / Larva: milkweed plants (*Asclepias*)		

MONARCH BUTTERFLY

FAMILY NYMPHALIDAE

Monarch butterflies are famous for their annual migrations that span several generations. In the fall, some of them fly up to 3,000 miles (4,800 km), from Canada to Mexico.

The generation that emerges in the fall doesn't mature into adulthood until it completes its migration. Then it takes about three or four generations in spring and summer to complete the northward journey.

Imagine: The butterflies that make the long migration south to Mexico will follow the same path as generations before them, even though they have never made the journey before. (See the butterfly migration map on pp. 50–51.)

The adults feed on nectar and lay eggs on milkweed plants. Monarch caterpillars bite the main vein of the milkweed leaf in order to stop the flow of the sticky, milky sap while they eat. They gain their toxicity from chemicals in the milkweed leaves. They retain that defense as pupae and adults. The bright orange and black wing colors of the adults serve as warning signs to predatory birds.

HABITAT Meadows, gardens, and woodlands near host plants and nectar plants

RANGE Originally North, Central, and South America. Currently found in many countries.

POSTMAN

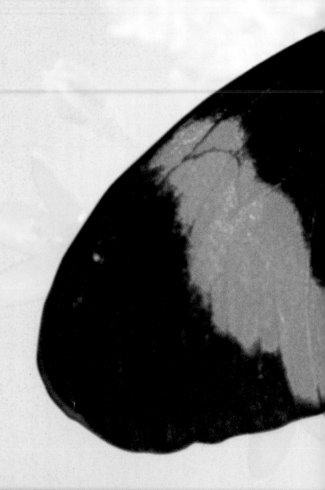

FAMILY HELICONIDAE

The postman and its relatives are remarkable and unique butterflies

for so many reasons. They sleep in groups among twigs and tendrils and tend to return each night to the same place. They feed on pollen in addition to nectar. The protein-rich pollen helps them to live long lives for an insect (up to a year) and to lay eggs throughout their lifetime. Also, they have flashy colors to warn predators that they are toxic. And they fly slowly as if to advertise their distastefulness.

The postman gets its toxicity from its host plants— passion vines—which are laced with the poison cyanide. The larvae break down the poison and re-form it into their own nasty chemicals. The postman shares its color pattern with a number of other butterflies and moths. That pattern warns birds not to eat them.

FACTS

OTHER COMMON NAME	Common postman	**SCIENTIFIC NAME**	*Heliconius melpomene* / Family: Heliconidae
SIZE	Wingspan about 2.17–3.15 inches (50–80 mm)	**WINGS**	Yes
FOOD	Adult: nectar and pollen / Larva: certain species of passion flower vines (*Passiflora*)		

Young birds that feed on butterflies must learn from experience what they can or can't eat. Distasteful butterflies like the postman sometimes fly around with battle scars from birds—beak-shaped bite marks on their wings. At least some butterflies are able to escape.

Two postman butterflies mating

HABITAT Rain forest

RANGE Central and northern South America

FACTS

COMMON NAME   Alcon blue

SCIENTIFIC NAME   *Phengaris alcon* / Family: Lycaenidae

FOOD   Adult: nectar / Larva: marsh gentian and willow gentian host plants, then regurgitated liquids from worker ants, and ant larvae and pupae

SIZE   Wingspan about 1.38 inches (35 mm)

WINGS   Yes

ALCON BLUE

FAMILY LYCAENIDAE

The alcon blue butterfly has an amazing story to tell: it's raised by ants.

Life for the alcon blue begins as a tiny white egg. After a few days, the caterpillar hatches and feeds on its host plant for about two weeks. Then it drops to the ground and waits to be discovered by aggressive *Myrmica* ants. Fooled by the smell of chemicals the caterpillar secretes, the ants passing by will mistake the caterpillar for one of their own and carry it back to their underground nest. There, worker ants will feed the caterpillar regurgitated liquids from their mouths (photo above). The caterpillar also feeds the ants sugary droplets secreted from a gland on its back. The relationship between the ants and caterpillars, however, is not always mutually beneficial. The caterpillar also eats the ants' young—without the adult ants objecting! This makes the alcon blue a nest parasite on the *Myrmica* ants. It pupates inside the ant nest, and once the adult emerges, it must quickly flee the nest—or be attacked. Then it begins this remarkable cycle all over again.

When the butterfly emerges from its pupal case, it no longer has the chemical protection it did as a caterpillar. But it's covered in lots of loose scales that drop off as the butterfly escapes the ant nest. The loose scales help to confuse the normally aggressive ants.

HABITAT   Where host plants and *Myrmica* ants live in the same place

RANGE   Most of Europe and northern Asia

DEAD LEAF BUTTERFLY

FAMILY NYMPHALIDAE

In flight, the dead leaf butterfly is spectacular

with its iridescent blue, orange, and black markings. But when it perches, it just plain disappears. With its wings closed, it's the spitting image of a dead leaf—right down to its veins. That's why it's called the dead leaf butterfly. The butterfly even flies so that it looks like a falling leaf. When it lands on the ground, it lies sideways and blends in with leaf litter.

Unlike most butterflies that are very similar in appearance among members of a species, the dead leaf varies a lot in the colors and pattern of dark splotches on the underside of its wings—even among siblings. For this reason, predatory birds can't memorize a particular "look," and this adds to the butterfly's incredible ability to blend in and hide.

FACTS

OTHER COMMON NAMES	Orange oakleaf butterfly, Indian leaf butterfly
SCIENTIFIC NAME	*Kallima inachus* / Family: Nymphalidae
FOOD	Adult: rotting fruit on the forest floor / Larva: leaves of plants in the knotweed family and a few others
SIZE	3.35–4.33 inches (85–110 mm)
WINGS	Yes

The dead leaf butterfly has two generations each year, one in the wet season and one in the dry season. (That means the first ones to lay eggs for the year will produce not just "children," but also "grandchildren" later that year.) The adults in the wet season emerge darker and smaller than the adults in the dry season.

HABITAT Tropical forests

RANGE Tropical parts of Asia, from India to Japan

FACTS

COMMON NAME Spicebush swallowtail

SCIENTIFIC NAME *Papilio troilus* / Family: Papilionidae

SIZE Wingspan about 3.5–4.5 inches (89–114 mm)

WINGS Yes

FOOD Adult: nectar and mineral-rich water / Larva: spicebush, sassafras, redbay

SPICEBUSH SWALLOWTAIL

FAMILY PAPILIONIDAE

Adult spicebush swallowtails are dark butterflies that fly low in wooded areas.

They flutter while visiting flowers like jewelweed and joe-pye weed. Sometimes they sip mineral-rich water from streams and wet soil. They readily group together with other species of butterflies when puddling. They also seek out mates and host plants to lay their eggs. Despite the fact that the adults are able to feed, they only tend to live between two days and two weeks.

To stay safe from predators, the larvae have several survival tricks. The caterpillars use silk to roll up part of a leaf, forming a shelter where they can't be seen by predators during the day. They come out to feed at night. The smallest caterpillars mimic bird droppings in their appearance. The larger ones have eyespots on their back (photo above). When disturbed, they tuck their head under their body, puff up their front end, and flash the big false "eyes" to scare off birds and other predators. They can also release a foul odor when disturbed.

When the female spicebush swallowtail is ready to lay eggs, she flies around checking out potential host plants. She uses her front legs to drum on the surface of different leaves. By doing this, she can taste if the plant is appropriate for her offspring. If so, she'll deposit her eggs on it.

HABITAT	Shady areas, especially in woodlands and woody swampland
RANGE	Eastern United States and southern Ontario, Canada

APOLLO BUTTERFLY

FAMILY PAPILIONIDAE

This gorgeous butterfly is highly prized by butterfly watchers and collectors. During the summer, it can be seen in flowery meadows in the Alps and other mountainous habitats in Europe. But it has been declining in numbers and disappearing from parts of its former range. Now it's considered in danger of extinction.

The apollo requires open meadows with nectar-producing flowers next to rocky outcrops, where they find their host plants. The female lays her eggs on the host, and the following spring, the caterpillars hatch out and eat the host's leaves. If one habitat, for example the meadow, is altered or destroyed, then the rocky outcrops aren't sufficient for the apollo butterfly to survive.

The apollo's habitat is gradually being replaced by agriculture, tree plantations, and buildings. Other serious problems in different locations include over-collecting and accidents with cars. Climate change may also be playing a role in the butterfly's demise. Now there are laws in various countries to protect the apollo. Conservationists are focusing their efforts on protecting the apollo's habitats and on raising and releasing butterflies into their natural environment.

FACTS

OTHER COMMON NAME	Mountain apollo
SCIENTIFIC NAME	*Parnassius apollo* / Family: Papilionidae
SIZE	Wingspan of about 2.75–3.5 inches (70–90 mm) / Females are larger than males
WINGS	Yes
FOOD	Adult: nectar / Larva: stonecrop (*Sedum* species) and houseleeks (*Sempervivum* species)

Individual butterflies of the same species tend to look alike. But some, like the apollo, have a lot of variation among themselves— such as in the number, size, and color of their spots.

HABITAT   Mountain meadows and pastures, and rocky outcrops

RANGE   Europe and central Asia

FACTS

COMMON NAME Common jezebel

SCIENTIFIC NAME *Delias eucharis* / Family: Pieridae

SIZE Wingspan of 2.5–3.35 inch (65–85 mm)

WINGS Yes

FOOD Adult: nectar / Larva: mistletoe (*Loranthus*)

COMMON JEZEBEL BUTTERFLY

FAMILY PIERIDAE

The jezebel flies high in the forest canopy, feeding on flower nectar. This species is dull on the upper side of the wings, but its underside explodes with bright colors—yellow, orange-red, black, and white. The bright colors advertise the jezebel's toxicity, which it gets from feeding on mistletoe plants as a caterpillar. When predatory birds see the colors, they know to avoid these butterflies.

Young caterpillars feed in dense clusters. When disturbed, they bungee jump from a silk thread formed by the silk gland on the underside of the head. They climb back up the thread when the coast is clear.

The males of many pierid butterflies, including the common jezebel, exhibit mud-puddling behavior. They gather together and drink mineral salts from puddles and moist soils.

HABITAT	Almost anywhere with trees, including gardens
RANGE	Wetter regions of India, Sri Lanka, Myanmar, and Thailand

BUTTERFLIES GALLERY

Butterflies have amazing wings made up of thousands of tiny scales.
These scales can be brightly colored or dull, and even transparent. Some butterflies have shiny, metallic colors, like the morpho.

Butterflies use their wing colors and patterns in many ways. They can be used for camouflage, to absorb heat, and to find a mate. Some toxic butterflies also rely on their bright colors to warn predators that they taste foul. Potential enemies, like birds, learn to keep away. With about 20,000 butterfly species, these fluttering insects live just about anywhere in the world. They can be found in rain forests, mountaintops, deserts, cities, and even your own backyard. Do you have a favorite of the species shown here?

Cairns birdwing is Australia's largest native butterfly. It inhabits the rain forests of Queensland on the northeast coast.

A small skipper butterfly rests at attention on a flower stalk. Skippers have strong wing muscles for darting in flight.

The peacock butterfly lives in Europe and parts of Asia. Its flashy eyespots may help deter predation. Adult butterflies hibernate over the winter.

A Malayan zebra butterfly drinks from moist, rocky soil. In Southeast Asia, these butterflies are often seen mud-puddling with other butterflies.

A close-up of a butterfly's iridescent wing scales. The optically formed colors that you see depend on the angle at which you look at the wings.

This cattleheart butterfly from Jamaica is a type of swallowtail butterfly. Its fuzzy thorax is covered in tightly packed black and red hairs.

233

In China the name of the atlas moth translates to "Snake's Head," due to the extensions on the tips of their forewings, which strongly resemble a snake's head.

FACTS

COMMON NAME   Atlas moth

SCIENTIFIC NAME   *Attacus atlas* / Family: Saturniidae

SIZE   Wingspan sometimes more than 10 inches (250 mm)

WINGS   Yes

FOOD   Adult: doesn't feed / Larva: leaves of certain citrus and other evergreen trees

ATLAS MOTH

FAMILY SATURNIIDAE

The atlas moth is one of the largest moths in the world. Its wingspan is almost one foot wide (30 cm) and the surface area of its wings is about 62 square inches (4,000 sq. mm). That's about the size of this page turned sideways.

These spectacular moths are hard to find in the wild. For one thing, they fly at night. Also, the adults have no proboscis for feeding, so they don't live long. They might last a week or two off their fat reserves. That means they have limited time to mate and lay eggs. The male can fly a couple of miles or more, using his feathery antennae to pursue a female's powerful, airborne pheromone (scent) trail.

The atlas moth is in the silk moth family. The caterpillars make a cocoon with a strong, brownish silk. In Taiwan, empty cocoons are used as small change purses.

HABITAT	Tropical and subtropical forests and shrublands
RANGE	Southeast Asia, especially across the Malay archipelago

LOBSTER MOTH

FAMILY NOTODONTIDAE

The caterpillars of the lobster moth are bizarre-looking, and they change their appearance as they grow. When a caterpillar hatches from its egg, it feeds on its eggshell and looks like an ant or spider with spindly legs. It even moves like an ant. It guards its eggshell and viciously attacks intruders. After the first molt, it switches to feeding on leaves of its host plants. With each successive molt, it develops an unusual-shaped body with a large head and tail end—eventually looking much like a lobster. It has two attachments on the end of its abdomen that are really caterpillar legs. When the caterpillar is disturbed by predators, it reaches out with its long front legs and throws its head back in a menacing display.

The caterpillar makes a strong cocoon and transforms into a pupa where it stays for the winter. It emerges as a brown, furry-looking adult in the spring.

FACTS

OTHER COMMON NAME	Lobster prominent	**SCIENTIFIC NAME**	*Stauropus fagi* / Family: Notodontidae
SIZE	Wingspan of 1.6–2.75 inches (40–70 mm)	**WINGS**	Yes
FOOD	Adult: may not feed / Larva: leaves of oak, beech, birch trees, or hazel		

The lobster moth belongs to a family that has some bizarre-looking caterpillars with humps, bumps, and spines. When they're not feeding, they often rest with their front and back ends raised.

HABITAT Woodlands

RANGE Europe, northern parts of Asia, up to the Arctic

FACTS

COMMON NAME	Bogong moth	**SCIENTIFIC NAME**	*Agrotis infusa* / Family: Noctuidae
SIZE	Wingspan of about 1.6–2.0 inches (40–50 mm)	**WINGS**	Yes
FOOD	Adult: nectar / Larva: grasses and forbs, including crop plants		

BOGONG MOTH

FAMILY NOCTUIDAE

Bogong moths can't stand the heat.

Each spring, when the temperature begins to rise, the moths leave their home in the wheat-growing areas of Queensland, Australia. They head south for the Australian Alps, where the climate is cool. They can journey more than 620 miles (1,000 km) on their migration.

The moths travel in huge numbers, and make pit stops on rocks, buildings, and trees. At rest, their wings overlap like a tiled roof. Bogongs fly at night and are attracted to city lights. They also visit flowers by day for nectar.

When they reach their destination in the mountains, the bogongs sleep through the summer in cool caves and dark crevices without feeding. During the fall they return northward to feed and breed.

Inside caves that are located in the bogongs' mountainous retreats, dead moths—accumulated over thousands of years—carpet the floor more than six feet (1.8 m) deep.

HABITAT Changes over the year with their migrations

RANGE Southern Australia

MORGAN'S SPHINX MOTH

There are about 1,450 species of sphinx moths. They hover when they visit flowers for nectar.

FAMILY SPHINGIDAE

The Morgan's sphinx moth has the longest proboscis of any moth—up to 14 inches (355 mm) long. Its proboscis is three times longer than its body!

The famous naturalist Charles Darwin never got to see this moth, but he predicted its existence. He received a package of orchids from Madagascar that startled him. Each flower had a nectar spur that was extremely long—up to 14 inches. Darwin wrote that in order for an insect to drink nectar from it, it would need an equally long proboscis. He predicted that a moth of that description would be the pollinator. As it drank nectar, it would get pollen rubbed onto its head, and then the moth would pollinate other flowers it visited.

Darwin got it right. The Morgan's sphinx moth flies up close to the orchid to give it a sniff, and then backs up and unrolls its large proboscis, before plunging it in to the orchid's nectar spur. The moth hovers like a hummingbird while it drinks, balancing itself against the flower with its front legs.

FACTS

OTHER COMMON NAME	Morgan's Sphinx hawk moth	**SCIENTIFIC NAME**	*Xanthopan morgani* / Family: Sphingidae	
SIZE	Wingspan of 5–6 inches (130–150 mm) / Proboscis up to 14 inches (355 mm)		**WINGS**	Yes
FOOD	Adult: nectar from *Angraecum sesquipedale* / Larva: leaves of wild custard-apple, soursop, and a few other plants			

HABITAT   Rain forest in eastern Madagascar

RANGE   East Africa and Madagascar

FACTS

COMMON NAME	Madagascan sunset moth	**SCIENTIFIC NAME**	*Chrysiridia rhipheus* / Family: Uraniidae
SIZE	Wingspan of 2.75–3.5 inches (70–90 mm)	**WINGS**	Yes
FOOD	Adult: nectar / Larva: *Omphalea* leaves		

MADAGASCAN SUNSET MOTH

FAMILY URANIIDAE

It's easy to think the Madagascan sunset moth is a butterfly. The wings have tails like a swallowtail butterfly, and it's so colorful. But the beautiful iridescence of its wings is an optical illusion. The color shifts as you look at it from different angles.

The females lay their eggs on toxic tropical host plants of the genus *Omphalea*. The toxins don't hurt the caterpillar, but help it to avoid predators throughout its life. The host plants live mainly near the east and west coasts of Madagascar. When the western host plants are hit by drought, the moths migrate to *Omphalea* trees in eastern Madagascar in order to survive. (See the section on migration on pp. 50-51.)

Not all moths in this family are day fliers like the Madagascan sunset moth. The ones that fly by day tend to have bright colors, but the ones that fly at night tend to be drab.

During the Victorian era (1837 to 1901), people used the wings of the Madagascan sunset moth to make jewelry.

HABITAT	Dry areas on the west coast and rain forest on the east coast
RANGE	Madagascar

EASTERN TENT CATERPILLAR MOTH

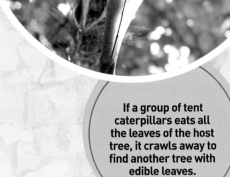

FAMILY LASIOCAMPIDAE

Eastern tent caterpillars hatch from a mass of eggs in the early spring. A single group may include up to 300 caterpillars!

After hatching, the caterpillars work together to make a silk tent in the tree branches where they live. The broad side of the tent faces the sun and helps to keep the caterpillars warm on cold days. As they grow, they add more layers of silk to enlarge the tent. Caterpillars often huddle inside; they may also sit on the outside to bask in the sun. When they're hungry, they leave their tent and "follow the leader" out to the branch tips to eat the leaves. If ants, birds, or other predators should disturb them, they rear up and thrash back and forth—all in unison! Their bodies are covered in bristles that can irritate predators. They can also retreat to the safety of their tent.

If a group of tent caterpillars eats all the leaves of the host tree, it crawls away to find another tree with edible leaves.

FACTS

OTHER COMMON NAMES	Tent moth, tent caterpillar
SCIENTIFIC NAME	*Malacosoma americanum* / Family: Lasiocampidae
FOOD	Adult: doesn't feed / Larva: cherry, apple, plum, peach, and hawthorn trees
SIZE	Wingspan of about 1 inch (25 mm)
WINGS	Yes

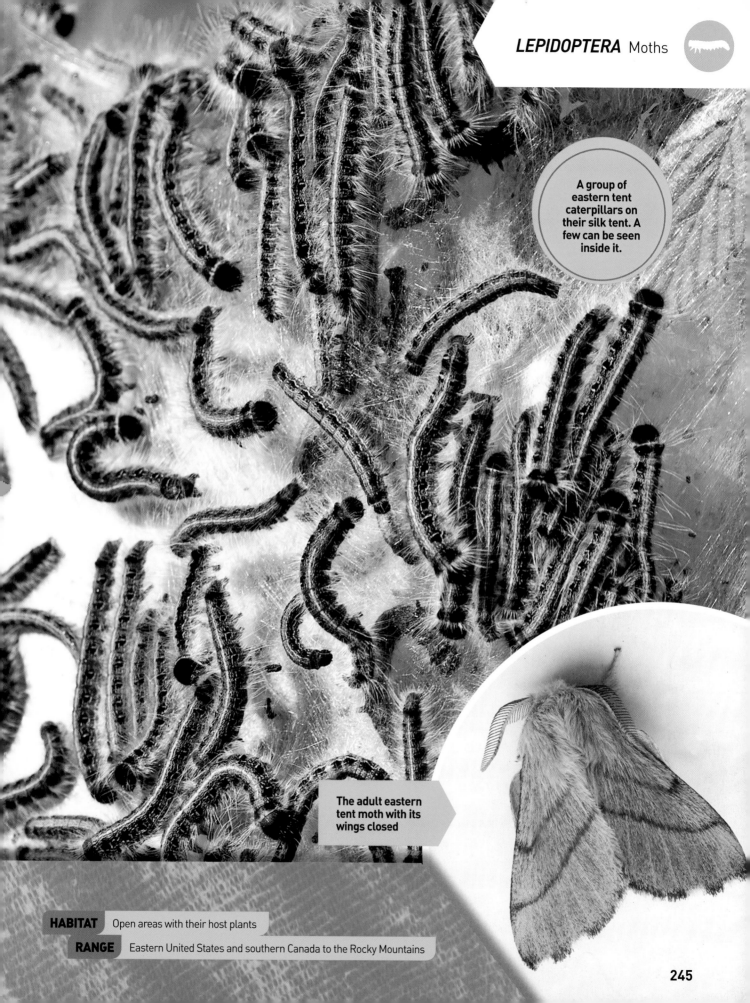

A group of eastern tent caterpillars on their silk tent. A few can be seen inside it.

The adult eastern tent moth with its wings closed

HABITAT   Open areas with their host plants

RANGE   Eastern United States and southern Canada to the Rocky Mountains

FACTS

TEAR-DRINKING MOTH

FAMILY NOLIDAE

Tear-drinking moths have a very special diet. They feed on tears—mainly of zebus and other large hoofed mammals.

Zebus are a common type of cattle in several southeast Asian countries. At night, tear-drinking moths fly to a zebu and line up around the rim of its eyes. They stick their proboscis into the animal's eye to drink up its tears. Tears are made up of water, salts, and some protein—enough to sustain small moths. If the zebu doesn't have moist eyes, no problem—the moth sweeps its spine-tipped proboscis across the eyeball to irritate it so that it makes more tears. If the zebu is sleeping with closed eyes, still no problem—the moth plunges its proboscis between the closed lids.

There are just over one hundred known species of moths from several different families that specialize in drinking tears. One that feeds on elephant tears in Thailand is aptly named the elephant-tear moth.

Like tear-drinking moths, the vampire moth (*Calyptra eustrigata*) has a very specialized diet: It drinks blood from mammals, including people. But unlike blood-drinking female mosquitoes, only the male vampire moths drink blood. In the photo above, the vampire moth is drinking blood from the furry back of a tapir.

HABITAT	Near livestock
RANGE	Myanmar, Thailand, and Cambodia

MORE ABOUT BUGS

Red-banded leafhopper

Colorado potato beetle larva on a potato leaf

Argiope spider in its web

Adult two-lined spittlebug in a frothy mass

Puss moth caterpillar in a defensive posture

Spoonwing, a relative of the antlion

249

A TALK WITH ENTOMOLOGIST BILL LAMP

Entomologists are scientists who study insects and arachnids. There are many different types of entomologists. Some research the adaptations and habitats of certain insects to learn more about them. And some identify ways to help conserve insects that are endangered.

Bill Lamp is an entomologist at the University of Maryland in College Park, Maryland. We spoke to Bill to learn more about what entomologists like him do, and to get some bug-studying tips.

Potato leafhopper nymph (Empoasca fabae) on alfalfa

Potato leafhoppers are insects that migrate to areas where food is abundant. They feed on the leaves of many different crops, such as potato, alfalfa, clover, soybeans, strawberries, and eggplant. The leafhoppers use a sharp mouthpart called a stylet to pierce the plants, and they produce saliva as they feed. Together, these two factors cause the leaves to brown. The effect is sometimes called "hopperburn."

What do entomologists do?

The range of study by entomologists is vast. Just to give a few examples, some of us study pollination of flowers by insects. Others study medically important insects, such as malaria-bearing mosquitoes, while others discover new species of insects around the globe. And still others specialize in pest management.

Tell us more about what you do.

I have a diverse research program that includes both aquatic insects and insects that feed on plants. My students and I have published papers on mayflies, caddisflies, and aquatic beetles from streams and wetlands. My major focus has been on sap-feeding insects such as leafhoppers and stink bugs, because of their ability to injure agriculturally important plants.

What inspired you to become an entomologist?

During college, I signed up to take an aquatic entomology course at the Lake Itasca Biology Station in Minnesota. On our first day, our professor took us to the headwaters of the Mississippi River. We collected insects from the stream, under stones, on branches, and along the edges. I was fascinated by all that I saw and later learned about aquatic insects.

What's your favorite insect?

 My favorite insect is *Anax junius,* the green darner dragonfly. In the larval (or nymph) stage, it is a voracious predator while it sits and waits for an unassuming fish or tadpole to pass by. Its lowest mouthparts reach out and grab its prey, and then bring it up to its sharp and deadly mandibles to eat.

 What advice would you give kids who want to study insects?

 The easiest way to collect insects to temporarily study them is with a simple sweep net—you just sweep up some grass or plants and then place the contents into a jar or cage, or even a sealable plastic bag. Then take a look to see if there are any insects inside. Once you spot them, release them and watch them carefully in nature to see what they might be doing.

 When you get up close to an insect, what do you look at or for?

 Observing the wings is good, like their number, size, and texture, because they are often used for identification. For example, a stinging bee has four wings, but a fly that mimics the bee and pretends to sting only has two.

 How much time do you spend studying a particular insect?

 I have studied the potato leafhopper, *Empoasca fabae,* since 1980—over 30 years! Other insects I've studied are stink bugs, aquatic beetles, mayflies, and caddisflies.

 Have you ever discovered an insect?

I did discover a fly that was new to North America. I was identifying insects that feed on thistle plants, and I raised the adult fly from larvae that fed on the roots of the thistle. A fly expert at the United States Department of Agriculture (USDA) identified the fly for me as a species that came from Europe.

 What tips can you offer for kids who want to observe insects in their backyard or at a nearby park or pond?

There are hundreds of species of insects that occur in a backyard over the course of a year. I would recommend that you keep your eyes open for any opportunity to find insects. Many are attracted to lights, so around porch lights is a great place. Insects like moist, dark places, so under fallen logs is a good place too. If you take a careful look at plants, the soil surface, flowers, or along streams and ponds, you will likely find insects there as well.

 How should kids handle insects they observe?

 It's okay to keep an insect for a short period of time if you're planning to observe certain behaviors, such as feeding and adult emergence. But be careful! Insects are easily injured by handling. Be aware that some insects sting or bite. You can tell by their [bright] coloration that they're dangerous. So keep a safe distance during this time. After you're done with your observation, release them back into the environment.

HOW YOU CAN HELP

According to the IUCN (the International Union for the Conservation of Nature), more than 4,000 species of insects are in danger of becoming extinct. What can you do to help?

Create a Butterfly Garden

Create a safe haven for butterflies by encouraging your family or school to plant a butterfly garden. What can you include in your garden? Brightly colored and strong-scented flowers, such as butterfly weed, lantana, and zinnias. These flowers not only attract butterflies, but they also contain nectar, which is an important food source. You'll also want to stock your garden with host plants where butterflies can lay their eggs. Some examples of host plants are milkweed, willow, and fennel. For more information about butterfly gardens, check out the Butterfly Conservation Initiative's resource page at www.butterflyrecovery. org/butterfly-resources.

Plant a Bee Garden

Bees need nectar and pollen from plants to survive. But with land development increasing, places for bees to find the right plants is decreasing. You can help by encouraging your family and friends to plant a bee garden. To get started, go to your local gardening store for plants that bees prefer, such as daisies, sunflowers, mint, and marigolds. These flowers produce lots of nectar. If you plant different types of seeds that grow in different seasons, your garden will bloom for most of the year. After planting, avoid using fertilizers and pesticides, which can harm bees. Also, bees drink water, so place a shallow container filled with water in your garden. Add some twigs to give the bees something to rest on as they sip. For more bee garden tips, go to http://thehoneybeeconservancy.org/act-today-2/plant-a-bee-garden.

Become a Ladybug Detective

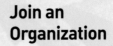

Ladybugs are well-loved predators that feast on small pests that harm plants. But throughout the United States, many ladybug species have gone missing over the years. At first, scientists thought that their populations had died out, but in fact, some of the ladybugs had just moved to a different place. Why? No one knows for sure, but an increase in non-native species to their habitat—which forces the native species to move elsewhere in search of food—may be one reason. Scientists have discovered missing ladybugs with the help of the Lost Ladybug Project. The project encourages interested helpers, like you, to take a photo of any ladybug they see and upload it to the project's website: http://lostladybug.org. Scientists then examine the photo to determine if the ladybug in the photo is a missing species.

Use Compost

Some fertilizers contain pesticides and other chemicals that can be harmful to insects and other wildlife. Encourage your family to ditch these harmful products in favor of compost. Compost is rotting organic matter, like grass clippings, leaves, and leftover food scraps such as apple cores, eggshells, and bread crumbs. When this rotting matter is mixed with soil, organisms such as beetles, bacteria, fungi, and other organisms will break down the compost. This releases nutrients into the soil and helps plants grow. And most important, compost is harmless to wildlife.

Join an Organization

Spreading the news about endangered insects raises public awareness about the matter. Educate yourself by joining a group like the Xerces Society (www.xerces.org), which publishes information about endangered insects and offers tips on how to help.

Curb Global Climate Change

According to scientists, burning fossil fuels, like oil and gasoline, releases heat-trapping gases into the atmosphere. The result is global climate change—a change in Earth's climate. This phenomenon threatens insects in many ways. For example, it makes it difficult for plants, which some insects use as food and shelter, to grow. You can help reduce the burning of fossil fuels by turning off the lights when you leave a room, replacing traditional light bulbs with fluorescent bulbs, putting on a sweater instead of turning up the heat, and towel drying your hair instead of blow-drying it.

Pick Up the Trash

Water pollution can make it hard for some water-dwelling insects to breathe and find food, while ground litter can make it difficult for trees and other plants—sources of shelter and food for many insects—to grow. So help keep your neighborhood, forests, and parks clean. Put on a pair of gloves to pick up trash and discourage "litter bugs" from doing further damage. If you can't discard larger items, such as tires and bins, be sure to empty them of any rainwater that collects inside. Reducing standing water, where mosquitoes breed, will help control their population.

SPIDERS

Daddy longlegs spider, also called a cellar spider

Pink and white crab spider poised to ambush an unsuspecting insect

A Hawaiian happy-face spider guarding her eggs

Jumping spider

A greenbottle blue tarantula, walking across moss

Southern black widow spider

255

ONE OF INSECTS' CLOSEST RELATIVES

Spiders may seem like insects, but they're actually arachnids—a class of invertebrate animals that includes scorpions, ticks, and mites. Unlike insects, which have three body parts, arachnids have only two: the cephalothorax (head and thorax combined) and the abdomen. They have eight legs, while insects have six. Also, arachnids lack the wings, antennae, and compound eyes that insects have. Instead, they typically have eight simple eyes. Spiders, like insects, can be found almost anywhere in the world, except for Antarctica.

With the exception of one vegetarian species in South America, all spiders are meat-eating carnivores. They eat insects such as moths, crickets, and flies. Some species even eat larger animals such as birds and frogs.

To catch their prey, different spiders have different methods. Some hunt down and grab their victim. Some hide out and ambush it. Others build webs by using the spinnerets on their abdomen. Depending on the species, spiderwebs can have various shapes, like orbs, funnels, and sheets.

Once they catch a meal, spiders must immobilize their prey. Many spiders inject venom from their fangs to paralyze it. Some, especially ones with short fangs, wrap their prey tightly in silk instead.

When it's time to eat, spiders either inject digestive juices with their fangs or secrete the juices from their jaws. The digestive juices break down the prey's tissues. When the tissues become a liquid, the spider slurps it up. Some larger spiders, such as tarantulas, have prominent teeth for tearing and grinding up their prey.

Check out a few of the almost 44,000 spider species shown here and on the next two gallery pages.

LEGS

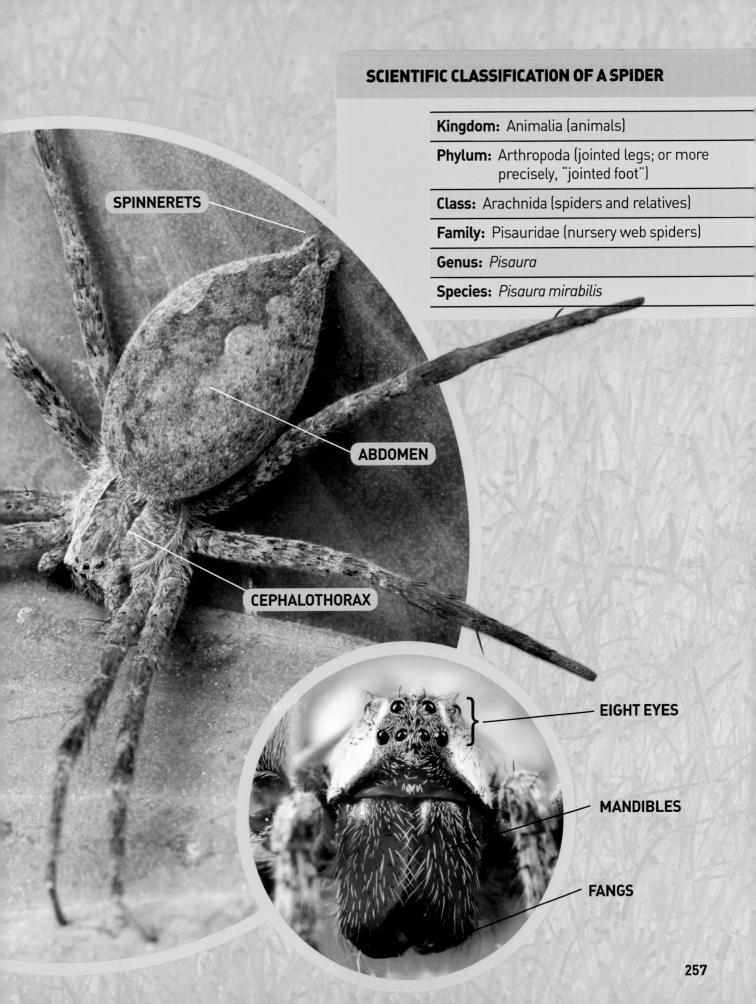

SPINNERETS

ABDOMEN

CEPHALOTHORAX

EIGHT EYES

MANDIBLES

FANGS

SCIENTIFIC CLASSIFICATION OF A SPIDER

Kingdom: Animalia (animals)

Phylum: Arthropoda (jointed legs; or more precisely, "jointed foot")

Class: Arachnida (spiders and relatives)

Family: Pisauridae (nursery web spiders)

Genus: *Pisaura*

Species: *Pisaura mirabilis*

SPIDERS GALLERY

This spider is releasing silk in order to loft itself.

A male peacock spider dances to attract a mate.

The ant-mimicking jumping spider looks and acts like an ant.

A wolf spider with a fly in its huge jaws. Wolf spiders are members of the family Lycosidae.

This leggy huntsman spider doesn't build webs; instead it relies on its incredible speed to catch prey.

A nursery web spider attacking a dragonfly

A goldenrod crab spider is visible against purple flowers, but on goldenrod plants, it's hard to find.

GLOSSARY

ADAPTATION – a feature that helps a living organism survive in its environment

ALGAE – simple, plantlike organisms that contain a green pigment color, but lack true stems, roots, and leaves. Algae range in size from single-celled species to giant kelp. They can live in fresh water or salt water and in moist places on land.

AQUATIC INSECTS – insects that spend part or all of their life in fresh water

BIOLUMINESCENCE – the production of light by a living organism

CAMOUFLAGE – an organism's ability to disguise its appearance, often by using its coloring or body shape to blend in with its surroundings. An example is a stick insect that looks just like a stick.

CARCASS – the dead body of an animal

CARNIVORE – an organism that eats meat. For example, insects that eat other insects are carnivores.

CARRION – the decaying flesh of a dead animal

COLONY – a group of the same kind of organism living or growing together. In social insects, such as leafcutter ants, colonies are typically large extended families.

COMMON NAME – the non-scientific name of an organism that is used by a community of people. Not all common names are the same in all regions. For example, a "buff-tailed bumblebee" in one region may be known as a "large earth bumblebee" in another.

COURTSHIP – a behavior used by animals to attract each other for mating

DEFENSE – a means by which an organism protects itself from attack or harm. Defenses can be part of an animal's body (for example, its spines), part of its coloring, part of its chemistry (an insect may be able to squirt acid, for instance) or its behavior (it can hide).

DEFOLIATE – to remove leaves from a plant, such as when certain insects eat the leaves

EGG CASE – a capsule that contains eggs. In certain insects, the mother makes a silk case (or capsule) that surrounds her fertilized eggs and protects them until they hatch.

ELYTRA – the hardened forewings, or wing covers, of certain insects, especially beetles. The elytra protect the functioning hind wings.

ENDANGERED – relating to an animal or plant that is found in such small numbers that it is at risk of becoming extinct, or no longer existing

ENVIRONMENT – the natural features of a place, such as its weather, the kind of land it has, and the type of plants that grow in it

EXTINCTION – the state of no longer existing, or being alive. When all the members of a species die out, they are said to go extinct.

EYESPOT– a round marking resembling an eye, such as a spot that appears on the wings of some butterflies. In some organisms, eyespots are a form of **mimicry.** An individual of a species will recognize other individuals of its species by its eyespots and other unique color patterns.

FOLIAGE – a cluster of leaves on a plant, tree, vine, or shrub. Also, the leaves of all plants in an area. An example of its use is in the term "fall foliage."

FORAGE – to search widely for food

FOREWINGS – the two front wings of a four-winged insect

FOSSIL – the preserved remains or traces of an organism that lived a long time ago

FUNGUS –an organism that produces spores and feeds on **organic matter.** Many species of fungi produce fruiting bodies called mushrooms, which release the spores when they mature.

GENERATION – all of the insects of a species that were hatched at about the same time. Some insects, especially social insects (like termites and ants), have overlapping generations, meaning that their young are continually being produced.

HABITAT – a place in nature where an organism lives throughout the year, or for shorter periods of time

HIND WINGS – the two back wings of a four-winged insect

HONEYDEW – a sweet, sticky substance that some insects, such as aphids and some bugs, secrete from their abdomens

HOST – an organism that a **parasite** feeds on. The parasite/host relationship is different from a **predator/prey** relationship. Typically, prey are killed and fed upon by a predator, whereas a host is somewhat hurt or disabled by its parasite. However,

if a "host" is attacked by a **parasitoid**, it is fed on gradually, and eventually it dies.

HOST PLANT – a species of plant that an insect or other organism depends on, usually as a source of food. For example, milkweeds are the host plants for monarch butterfly caterpillars.

INSECT CLASSIFICATION – The grouping of insects based on their relatedness and their physical characteristics. For example, the class Insecta (insects) is divided into orders (such as Diptera, or flies). The order is divided into families. Each family is divided into genera (the plural of genus), and each genus is divided into species. (In some cases, there is only one member of a family or genus.) The species has a double name that is italicized. The first name is the genus name followed by a specific name.

INVASIVE SPECIES – species that are introduced accidentally or on purpose from their native habitat to a new location. Also called "introduced species" or "exotic species." Invasive species typically have a bad effect on native plants and animals.

INVERTEBRATE – an organism without a backbone. Invertebrates include insects, arachnids, crustaceans, and mollusks.

IRIDESCENT – displaying rainbow-like colors that change when seen from different angles. The wings of a Madagascan sunset moth are an example.

LARVA (plural: **larvae**) – an immature form of an insect with complete **metamorphosis**. Larvae have alternative names such as caterpillars (for butterflies and moths), grubs (for beetles, bees, and wasps), maggots (for flies), and wrigglers (for mosquitoes). In the process of metamorphosis, the larva becomes the pupa, and then the adult.

LUCIFERASE – a particular enzyme (substance) produced in bioluminescent organisms, such as fireflies and glowworms, to make light.

MANDIBLES – in insects, crustaceans, and centipedes, a pair of appendages, or jaws, used mainly for tearing and chewing food, and for carrying objects. Some insects, such as butterflies and most moths, lack mandibles as adults, but their larvae have them.

MEASUREMENT – the length, height, or width of something. In most areas of the world, the metric system is the preferred system of measurement, while in the United States, U.S. standard units are used. Some common units of measurement include:
  1 millimeter (mm) = .04 inches (in.)
  1 centimeter (cm) = .4 inches (in.)
  1 meter (m) = 3.3 feet (ft.)
  1 kilometer (km) = 3,281 feet (ft.)
  1 gram = .04 ounces (oz.)
  1 kilogram (kg) = 2.2 pounds (lb.)

METAMORPHOSIS – in insects, it is the process of changing from an immature form to an adult form. Insects with simple metamorphosis go from egg to nymph to adult. Those with complete metamorphosis go from egg to larva to pupa to adult.

MIGRATION – in insects, the seasonal movement from one location to another. The migration may be prompted by various environmental cues, including weather and availability of food. Monarch butterflies and bogong moths are examples of insects that migrate.

MIMICRY – the similarity of one species to another (or others) that can act to protect one or more species. The similarity might not be just in appearance, but also in sounds, smells, or behavior. Butterflies with nearly identical wing color patterns are often said to exhibit mimicry.

MOTTLED – covered with spots or having colored areas

MUD-PUDDLING – a behavior mostly seen in butterflies, in which they drink from wet soil to obtain moisture and nutrients. Butterflies can often be seen mud-puddling in groups.

NECTAR – a sweet liquid secreted by plants as food to attract animals that will benefit them. Many flowers produce nectar to attract pollinating insects, birds, and bats. Nectar consists primarily of water and sugars, including fructose, glucose, and sucrose.

NYMPH – the immature form of an insect with simple **metamorphosis**. The nymphs of flying insects have wing buds on their back, unlike **larvae,** which start to develop wings inside the **pupa**. Nymphs look like smaller versions of the adult, and often feed on the same type of food.

ORGANIC MATERIAL – matter that remains of dead plants and animals and their waste products

OVIPOSITOR – the egg-laying organ on a female insect and some other animals. In some insects, the ovipositor is also used to burrow into soil or plant tissues, or to pierce wood prior to laying eggs. Certain wasps, bees, and ants use their ovipositor as a stinger.

PARASITE – an insect (or any organism) that lives on or inside another species of organism (the **host**) and feeds on it. Generally, a parasite does not kill the host. But a form of parasite called a **parasitoid** grows up feeding on its live host, which eventually kills the host. Many types of organisms can be considered parasitoids, but of the insect parasitoids, the most common are certain wasps and flies.

PHEROMONE – an airborne chemical secreted by an insect (or other animal) that influences the behavior of other members of the same species. Certain pheromones can attract mates, others can be used to sound the alarm to nest-mates, and still others can be used to mark a trail to food sources. Pheromones are a form of chemical communication.

POLLEN – tiny grains produced by the male part of flowers that fertilize the future seeds of a plant of the same species. Many plants recruit insects (known as pollinators) to carry the pollen from one flower or plant to another in the process of pollination.

PREDATOR – an animal that hunts other animals for food. Its behavior is "predatory."

PREY – an animal that is hunted and eaten by other animals

PROBOSCIS – in insects, the elongated tubular mouthparts for drinking a liquid meal

PRONOTUM – a hardened plate on the top of the thorax just behind the head of insects. The pronotum is part of the insect's exoskeleton. Treehoppers, for example, have exceptionally large pronotums compared to the rest of their body.

PUPA (plural: **pupae**) – a life stage of insects with complete **metamorphosis** during which the larval body is replaced with an adult body. Although the pupa is generally immobile, it undergoes tremendous changes on the inside. The pupa is enclosed in a cocoon in certain insects. Other names for insect pupae are chrysalis (in butterflies) and tumblers (in mosquitoes).

RAIN FOREST – an evergreen forest with upwards of 160 inches (406 cm) of rain in a year. There are both **tropical** and **temperate** rain forests.

SCAVENGER – an animal (insect) that feeds on dead or decaying matter.

SCIENTIFIC NAME – a unique two-part name used by scientists to identify each type of organism. Most scientific names come from Latin or Greek. For example *Danaus plexippus* is the scientific name for the monarch butterfly. There are other related species of butterflies in the genus *Danaus* (each with a double name starting with *"Danaus"*), and in turn

they are part of the butterfly family Nymphalidae, which in turn is in the order Lepidoptera, which consists of all butterflies and moths.

SEDIMENTARY ROCK – rocks that are formed by the gradual depositing of soil, sand, minerals, or other loose material over the surface of the earth or over the bottom of bodies of water. Sedimentary rocks are deposited in layers that can be dated.

TEMPERATE ZONE – that part of the Earth's surface located between the tropics and the polar regions. The temperate zone is characterized by a warm summer and a cool winter.

TERRITORIAL – relating to animals that carefully guard an area considered to be their own. For example, a male giant helicopter damselfly guards a tree hole from other males, so that he is the one who gets the opportunity to mate with a female, who will then lay her eggs in the puddle of water inside the tree hole.

THORAX – the part of the body between the head and the abdomen. In insects, the wings and legs are attached to the thorax.

TOXICITY – the quality of being toxic or poisonous to an organism.

TRANSPARENT – allowing light to pass through, as in see-through.

TROPICAL ZONE – the part of the Earth's surface surrounding the Equator. The tropics are characterized by a hot climate year round.

TRUE BUGS – any insect in the order Hemiptera, such as aphids, assassin bugs, cicadas, and giant water bugs. True bugs have piercing and sucking mouthparts.

VERTEBRATE – an organism with a backbone. Vertebrates can include mammals, fish, reptiles, amphibians, and birds.

263

FIND OUT MORE

Great Websites, Movies, and Places to Visit

Websites

To find out more about insects and join a Bug Club, visit the Amateur Entomologists' Society website: www.amentsoc.org/bug-club

Need help identifying an insect? Visit the What's That Bug website: www.whatsthatbug.com

You can also figure out what bug you're looking at by visiting the Insect Identification website: www.insectidentification.org

To find tons of photos of insects and discussions about them, visit BugGuide's website: bugguide.net/node/view/15740

Insects and other mini-beasts are the stars on University of Kentucky's Critter Files website: www.uky.edu/Ag/CritterFiles/casefile/casefile.htm

To find out about the biggest and fastest insects and other record-holders in the bug world, check out the University of Florida's Book of Insect Records website: entomology.ifas.ufl.edu/walker/ufbir

For photos and facts, explore the Insects.org website: www.insects.org

Explore the world of butterflies and moths on The Butterflies and Moths of North America (BAMONA) project's website: www.butterfliesandmoths.org

For great information and photos of insects, visit National Geographic's "Bugs" website: animals.nationalgeographic.com/animals/bugs

Watch insect videos on BBC Nature's "Insects" website: www.bbc.co.uk/nature/life/Insect

To find information as well as jokes and activities about insects, visit Enchanted Learning: www.enchantedlearning.com/themes/insects.shtml

A world of insect exploration awaits on the website of the Entomological Society of America: www.entsoc.org

The insects of Australia come to life on the Australian Museum's website: australianmuseum.net.au/Insects

Movies

BBC

Life: Insects: Episode 6 in season one of this acclaimed series about life on Earth focuses on insects, taking viewers right into the hives of honeybees and showing the journeys of monarch butterflies.

Life in the Undergrowth (2006): The camera focuses on the hidden lives of insects, unfolding in secret all around us.

Microcosmos (1996): This documentary includes amazing close-up footage of small-scale events, such as the growth of a mosquito, and ants at work.

Nature

Alien Empire (1995): This documentary explores insect body structure, migration, and means of survival.

Silence of the Bees (2008): The disappearance of bees resulting from the mysterious condition known as colony collapse disorder is examined in this film.

NOVA

Ants: Little Creatures Who Run the World: This documentary explores the lives of ant species around the world.

Bees: Tales from the Hive: Dive right into a hive and see what it's like to be a honeybee.

The Incredible Journey of the Butterflies: This film tells about the amazing yearly migration of monarch butterflies.

The Unknown World: The camera gets close-up and personal with insects and other tiny creatures that live around us— and on us!

Places to Visit

U.S.A.:

Insect Zoo, Natural History Museum of Los Angeles County, California

University of Arkansas Arthropod Museum, Fayetteville, Arkansas

Insect Zoo, San Francisco Zoo, San Francisco, California

Bohart Museum of Entomology, Davis, California

The Butterfly Pavilion, Westminster, Colorado

Butterfly World, Coconut Creek, Florida

University of Georgia Insect Zoo, Athens, Georgia

K-State Insect Zoo, Manhattan, Kansas

Audubon Butterfly Garden and Insectarium, New Orleans, Louisiana

Butterfly House, Missouri Botanical Garden, Chesterfield, Missouri

Monsanto Insectarium, St. Louis Zoo, St. Louis, Missouri

Magic Wings Butterfly House and Bayer CropScience Insectarium, Museum of Life and Science, Durham, North Carolina

World of the Insect, Cincinnati Zoo, Cincinnati, Ohio

Insect Zoo, Oregon Zoo, Portland, Oregon

Brown Hall of Entomology and Cockrell Butterfly Center, Houston Museum of Natural Science, Houston, Texas

Insectropolis, Toms River, New Jersey

O. Orkin Insect Zoo, Butterfly Pavilion, Smithsonian National Museum of Natural History, Washington, D.C.

Invertebrate Exhibit, National Zoo, Washington, D.C.

Outside U.S.A.:
Canada

Insectarium de Quebec, Montreal, Quebec, Canada [espacepourlavie.ca/insectarium]

Victoria Butterfly Gardens, Brentwood Bay, British Columbia, Canada

Victoria Bug Zoo, Victoria, British Columbia, Canada

Lyman Entomological Museum and Research Laboratory, McGill University, Ste-Anne-de-Bellevue, Quebec, Canada

Niagara Parks Butterfly Conservatory, Niagara Falls, Ontario, Canada [www.niagaraparks.com/garden-trail/butterfly-conservatory.html]

Newfoundland Insectarium, Reidville, Newfoundland, Canada [www.nfinsectarium.com]

South/Central America

Shipstern Nature Reserve, Belize [It has a butterfly garden: www.shipstern.or]

The Butterfly Farm, La Guacima de Alajuela, Costa Rica [www.butterflyfarm.co.cr]

Europe

London Zoo, London, England [It has an insect house called BUGS (Biodiversity Underpinning Global Survival): www.zsl.org/zsl-london-zoo/exhibits/bugs]

Artis Royal Zoo, Amsterdam, Netherlands [It has a butterfly pavilion and insectariums: www.artis.nl/en/discover-artis/artis]

Cologne Zoological Garden, Cologne, Germany [It has an insectarium: www.koelnerzoo.de/zoo-tierwelten/aquarium/das-insektarium]

Budapest Zoo, Budapest, Hungary [It has insects and a butterfly pavilion: www.zoobudapest.com/english/species]

Welhelma Zoological and Botanic Garden, Stuttgart, Germany [It has an insectarium: www.wilhelma.de/ and specifically www.wilhelma.de/de/tiere-und-pflanzen/tiere/insektarium.html]

Bristol Zoo, Bristol, England [It has a bug world: www.bristolzoo.org.uk/bug-world]

Butterfly Park Benalmádena, Benalmádena, Malaga, Spain [www.mariposariodebenalmadena.com/English/index.html]

Micropolis, Aveyron, France [It has an insect museum: www.micropolis-aveyron.com]

Asia

Siam Insect-Zoo and Museum, Mae Rim, Thailand

Zoo Negara, Hulu Kelang, Selangor Darul Ehsan, Malaysia [It has an insect zoo with 200 species: www.zoonegaramalaysia.my]

Tama Zoo, Tokyo, Japan [It has an insectarium: www.tokyo-zoo.net/english/tama/main.html]

Penang Butterfly Farm, Penang, Malaysia [www.butterfly-insect.com]

Phuket Butterfly Garden and Insect World, Phuket, Thailand [www.phuketbutterfly.com]

Insectarium, Hiroshima City Forest Park, Hiroshima, Japan

Bangkok Butterfly Garden and Insectarium, Bangkok, Thailand

Africa

ButterflyWorld, Klapmuts, South Africa [www.butterflyworld.co.za]

Insectarium de la Reunion, Reunion [sciencesecole.ac-reunion.fr/html/insectes/insectarium.html]

Australia

Melbourne Museum, Melbourne, Australia [It has a Bugs Alive! permanent exhibit: museumvictoria.com.au/melbournemuseum/whatson/current-exhibitions/bugs-alive]

Royal Melbourne Zoological Park, Parkville, Victoria, Canada [It has a butterfly house and bug exhibit: www.zoo.org.au/melbourne]

INDEX

Boldface indicates illustrations.

INDEX

INDEX

PHOTO CREDITS

KEY: SS: Shutterstock; NGYS: National Geographic Your Shot; MP: Minden Pictures; NGS: National Geographic Stock; WK: Wikipedia

COVER: (background), Triff/SS; (milliaris), Alslutsky/SS; (blue beetle), Cosmin Manci/SS; (ants), Kesu/SS; (ladybugs), mehmet karaca/NGYS; (caterpillar), AnestSS; (pink moth), Kim Taylor/ naturepl.com; (monarch butterfly), SS; (blue butterfly), Marc Bruxelle/SS; (katydid), Dr. Arthur Anker; **SPINE:** (ant), Kesu/SS; (butterfly), SS; **FRONT FLAP:** (fly), Irin-K/SS; (beetle, Darlyne A. Murawski; (mosquito), Aynia Brennan/NGYS; **BACK COVER:** (butterfly), Ilker Canikligil/SS; (grasshopper), Chrom/SS; **BACK FLAP:** (Darlyne Murawski), Darlyne A. Murawski; (Nancy Honovich), Nicole Delma/FOND Group; (Dr. Bill Lamp), Dr. Bill Lamp; (bee on flower), Pamela Parr/NGYS; **FRONT MATTER:** 1, Stephen Dalton/MP; 2 (Background), Jirí Hodecek/SS; 2, Norbert Wu/MP; 3 (ant), Kesu/SS; 3 (wasp), irin-k/SS; 3 (ant), Kesu/SS; 3 (grasshopper), Eric Isselée/SS; 3 (beetle), Cosmin Manci/SS; 4, Tc Morgan/NGYS; 4, Bernadi Gunawan/NGYS; 4 (UPRT), Dietmar Nill/Foto Natura/MP; 4 (Background), Phil Thorogood/NGYS; 4 (LOLE), Fir0002/Flagstaffotos/WK; 4 (LORT), ku za/NGYS; 5 (CTR LE), Hendroh/SS; 5 (UPRT), johan botes/NGYS; 5 (CTR RT), Cathy Keifer/SS; 5 (LOLE), jen king/NGYS; 5 (LORT), Cathy Keifer/SS; 6 (Background), Triff/SS; 6 (UPRT), Dr. BIll Lamp; 6 (UP), Kesu/SS; 6 (CTR), alslutsky/SS; 6 (LOCTR), gosphotodesign/SS; 6 (LORT), irin-k/SS; 7 (UPLE), Darlyne A. Murawski; 7 (UPRT), mehmet karaca/NGYS; 7 (CTR), Darlyne A. Murawski; 7 (LORT), Darlyne A. Murawski; 7 (LOLE), Darlyne A. Murawski; 8 (Background), Triff/ SS; 10 (Background), Uri Kolker/NGYS; 10 (UPLE), Jim Johnson/ NGYS; 10 (UPRT), aditya Nugraha/NGYS; 10 (LORT), Mark Bridger/SS; 10 (LOLE), Eran Finkle/NGYS; 11 (LO), Tc Morgan/ NGYS; 11 (UPLE), Luca Barovier/NGYS; 12 (Background), Triff/SS; 12–13, thilak raman/NGYS; 12 (INSET), Caitlin Sanders/NGYS; 13 (RT), George Grall/NGS; 14–15 (Background), Triff/SS; 14, Sunny Dutta/NGYS; 15 (UPLE), Yvonne Metcalfe/NGYS; 15 (UPRT), Wasu Watcharadachaphong/SS; 15 (LO), asti amalina/NGYS; 16–17 (Background), Triff/SS; 16 (UP), John O Neill/NGYS; 16 (LO), Karen Cooper/NGYS; 17 (UP), Paul Zahl/NGS; 17 (LO), acob Benner-Tufts University/Reuters; 18–19 (Background), Triff/SS; 18 (UP), artcasta/SS; 18 (LO), Praveen Siddannavar/NGYS; 19 (UP), Vilainecrevette/SS; 19 (CTR), skynetphoto/SS; 19 (LO), Kletr/ SS; 20–21 (Background), Triff/SS; 21 (1), Mickey Alesch/NGYS; 21 (2), Volha Johnson/NGYS; 21 (3), Angela Klempner/NGYS; 21 (4), Ken Bower/NGYS; 21 (LOLE), Dwight R. Kuhn; 21 (LOCTR), Dwight R. Kuhn; 21 (LORT), All Canada Photos/Alamy; 22–23 (Background), Triff/SS; 22, Roman Teteruk/SS; 23 (CTR), Shalini Dhameja/NGYS; 23 (LO), Chandana Liyanage/NGYS; 23 (UP), Darren5907/Alamy; 24–25 (Background), Triff/SS; 24 (LE), seow hon tan/NGYS; 24 (RT), Rebecca Lashley/NGYS; 25 (UP), Ben Reynolds/NGYS; 25 (LOLE), Alice Schaub/NGYS; 25 (LORT), hwongcc/SS; 26–27 (Background), Triff/SS; 26 (LE), Kacey Arnold/ NGYS; 26 (RT), Andrea Erbeck/NGYS; 27 (UP), Melola/SS; 27 (LOLE), Shantanu Prasad/NGYS; 27 (LORT), Amir Ridhwan/SS; 28–29 (Background), Triff/SS; 28 (LE), Avinesh Singh/NGYS; 28 (RT), Digital Media Pro/SS; 28 (branches), andersphoto/SS; 29 (UP), Darlyne A. Murawski/NGS; 29, Matthias Lenke; 29 (LO), April Moore/NGYS; 30 (UPRT), Carol Milne/NGYS; 30 (LOLE), Henrik Larsson/SS; 30–31 (Background), Triff/SS; 30 (LORT), rachel sachse/NGYS; 31 (UPRT), Scott Holmes/NGYS; 31 (CTR), Colin Hutton/NGYS; 31 (LO), Theresa Wiltrout/NGYS; 31 (UPLE), Sarin Kunthong/SS; 32–33 (Background), Triff/SS; 32 (LO), Premkumar Antony/NGYS; 32–33, WK; 33 (RT), Radim Schreiber/ NGYS; 34–35 (Background), Triff/SS; 34, George Grall/NGS; 35 (UPRT), Mladen Bozickovic/NGYS; 35 (1), Eye Of Science/SPL/ Barcroft/Landov; 35 (2), Dwight R. Kuhn; 35 (3), Jadon Webb/ NGYS; 35 (4), Steve Gschmeissner/SPL/Barcroft/Landov; 35 (5), edemin ramirez/NGYS; 35 (6), Sunil Gopalan/NGYS; 35 (7), Marius Jursys/NGYS; 35 (8), Amit Bansal/NGYS; 35 (9), Mladen Bozickovic/NGYS; 35 (10), Dennis Kunkel Microscopy, Inc./Visuals Unlimited, Inc.; 36–37 (Background), Triff/SS; 36 (UP), joseph quinn/NGYS; 36–37 (branches), andersphoto/SS; 36 (LO), Ch›ien Lee/MP; 36–37 (Background), Triff/SS; 37 (UPRT), Carolyn Pepper/NGYS; 37 (CTR LE), Giancarlo Sherman/NGYS; 37 (CTR RT), Nigel Cattlin/Science Source; 37 (LOLE), Susan Schalbe/ NGYS; 37 (LORT), Diane Binford/NGYS; 37, Stephen Dalton/MP; 38–39, Triff/SS; 38, Karen Cusick/NGYS; 39 (UPLE), Timothy Lewis Bale/NGYS; 39 (CTR), Piotr Naskrecki/MP; 39 (UPRT), pamela parr/NGYS; 39 (LO), heather levingstone/NGYS; 40, vblinov/SS; 41 (LOLE), SergeylT/SS; 41 (LORT), Tan Hung Meng/ SS; 41 (UP CTR), Piotr Naskrecki/MP; 41 (UPLE), Piotr Naskrecki/ MP; 41 (UPRT), Piotr Naskrecki/MP; 42 (UP), Thomas Ames, Jr./ Visuals Unlimited, Inc.; 42 (LO), ilker canikligil/SS; 43 (UP), Javed Hossain/NGYS; 43, Kenneth Bart/Visuals Unlimited, Inc.; 43 (LO), al fizar/NGYS; 44 (LO), Satoshi Kuribayashi/Nature Production/ MP; 44 (UP), Craig Taylor/SS; 44–45, Triff/SS; 45 (UP), perry leaves/NGYS; 45 (LORT), julie maher/NGYS; 45 (LOLE), Linda Brewer/NGYS; 46–47, Triff/SS; 46 (UP), H M lindner/NGYS; 46 (LOLE), Leighton Reid/NGYS; 46 (LORT), kristi charnigo/NGYS; 47 (UPLE), bernadi gunawan/NGYS; 47 (UPRT), Norbert Wu/MP; 47 (CTR RT), Ciju Panicker Cherian/NGYS; 47 (LO), Ciju Panicker Cherian/NGYS; 48–49, Triff/SS; 48, Yojik/SS; 48 (LO), Babu AM/ NGYS; 49 (UP), Babu AM/NGYS; 49 (1), Babu AM/NGYS; 49 (2), blickwinkel/Alamy; 49 (3), Kristy Potter/NGYS; 49 (4), Ch'ien Lee/ MP; 49 (5), sumita roy/NGYS; 49 (6), Wiratchai wansamngam/SS; 49 (7), S.Picavet/Getty Images; 49 (8), hwongcc/SS; 49 (9), Dwight R. Kuhn; 49 (10), Maksimilian/SS; 52–53 (Background), Triff/SS; 52–53, Anthony Mercer/NGYS; 53 (UP), Darlyne A. Murawski/ NGS; 53 (LO), Matt Howard/SS; 54–55 (Background), Triff/SS; 54, Przemyslaw Wasilewski/SS; 55 (1), Stephane Bidouze/SS; 55 (2), Zeljko Radojko/SS; 55 (3), akiyoko/SS; 55 (4), WvdM/SS; 55 (5), Thor Jorgen Udvang/SS; 55 (6), Pavel L Photo and Video/SS; 55 (7), TSpider/SS; 55 (8), mycola/SS; 55 (9), Peter Gudella/SS; 55 (10), Carolina K. Smith MD/SS; **SIMPLE METAMORPHOSIS:** 56–57, Rachel Drummond/NGYS; 56 (LE), Piotr Naskrecki/MP; 56 (UPRT), Darlyne A. Murawski/NGS; 56 (LORT), Jessica Straw/ NGYS; 57 (UP), Michael Durham/MP; 57 (LO), Cory Bucher/NGYS; 58 (LE), Nigel Cattlin/Alamy; 58 (CTR), blickwinkel/Alamy; 58 (RT), Graham Montgomery; 58–59, Michael Walker/NGYS; 60, eric wright/NGYS; 60–61, Brett Colvin/NGYS; 61 (Background), Jakkrit Orrasri/SS; 62 (Background), Photodisc; 62, Jan Hamrsky/ naturepl.com; 63, Bob Jensen/Photoshot; 64 (INSET), Muhammad Mahdi Karim/WK; 64, Hans Hillewaert/ CC-BY-SA-3.0/WK; 65 (Background), lchumpitaz/SS; 66–67 (Background), Triff/SS; 66 (UP), Ajit Pal Singh/NGYS; 66 (LOLE), Rachel Godden/NGYS; 66 (LORT), James Reben/NGYS; 67 (UP), Tomas1111/SS; 67 (LOLE), Dharmaji VenuGopal/NGYS; 67 (LORT), Pamela Hastry/NGYS; 68, Mark Moffett/MP; 69, Steve Collins; 69 (Background), Photodisc; 70 (Background), iSIRIPONG/SS; 70, Fir0002/Flagstaffotos/WK; 71, Giedrius Zaleckas/NGYS; 72, Piotr Naskrecki/MP; 72, Piotr Naskrecki/MP; 73 (Background), Photodisc; 74 (Background), Visun Khankasem/SS; 74, Rhonda Simmons/NGYS; 75, Bartomeu Borrell/Collection/Photoshot; 76, Camillo Longo/NGYS; 77 (Background), Jakkrit Orrasri/SS; 77, Sonja Wedmann; 78 (Background), lchumpitaz/SS; 78, P.E. Bragg/ WK; 79, paul coleman/NGYS; 79 (Background), Photodisc; 80, Ulkastudio/SS; 81 (Background), Photodisc; 81, Fir0002/ Flagstaffotos/WK; 81 (Background), Photodisc; 82 (Background), iSIRIPONG/SS; 82, James H RobinsonPhoto Researchers RM/ Getty Images; 83, Pamela Wanamaker/NGYS; 84, Dietmar Nill/ Foto Natura/MP; 85 (Background), Digital Stock; 85, F1online digitale Bildagentur GmbH/Alamy; 86–87 (Background), Triff/SS; 86–87, Patrick Strutzenberger/NGYS; 86 (LE), Lisa Armstrong/ NGYS; 86 (LORT), Michael Herdman/NGYS; 87 (LOLE), meriniza nacu/NGYS; 87 (UPRT), Doug Lemke/SS; 87 (LORT), Chris Carvalho/NGYS; 88 (Background), Photodisc; 88, Justin Philip Lawrence/NGYS; 89, Mitsuhiko Imamori/MP; 90, Daniel Pedersen/NGYS; 91, Kristina Postnikova/SS; 91 (Background), Photodisc; 92–93 (Background), Triff/SS; 92–93, Thanh Ta Quang/ NGYS; 92 (LOLE), Thanh Ta Quang/NGYS; 92 (LORT), Flavio Leone/NGYS; 93 (UP), Robert Jensen/NGYS; 93 (LOLE), suhail mir/NGYS; 93 (LORT), Roger Meerts/SS; 94 (Background), Jakkrit Orrasri/SS; 94, Peter Essick/NGS; 95, Peter Essick/NGS; 95 (INSET), fritz16/SS; 96, Darlyne A. Murawshki/NGS; 97, anvita pauranik/NGYS; 97 (Background), Visun Khankasem/SS; 98 (Background), Photodisc; 98,/Frans Lanting/Mint Images/Getty Images; 99, Nigel Cattlin/FLPA; 100, Densey Clyne/AUSCAPE; 101 (Background), Digital Stock; 101, Bill Buchanan, U.S. Fish and Wildlife Service; 102 (Background), Photodisc; 102, Darlyne A. Murawski/NGS; 103, George Grall/NGS; 104–105 (Background), Triff/SS; 104–105, Nathan Cooper/NGYS; 104 (LOLE), Jason Wiles/NGYS; 104 (LORT), Darlyne A. Murawski/ NGS; 105 (UP), Steve Irvine/NGYS; 105 (LOLE), Caitlin Sanders/ NGYS; 105 (LORT), Lorne Rossman/NGYS; 106, Ingo Arndt/MP; 107 (LE), Darlyne A. Murawski/NGS; 107 (Background), Jakkrit Orrasri/SS; 107 (RT), Karl Gehring/The Denver Post/Getty Images; 108 (Background), iSIRIPONG/SS; 108, Kazuo Unno/ Nature Production/MP; 109, Mitsuhiko Imamori/MP; 110, Paul Zahl/NGS; 111 (Background), Photodisc; 111, Mitsuhiko Imamori/ MP; 112–113, Darlyne A. Murawski/NGS; 113 (INSET), Frank Vincentz/WK; 114, Mark Berkery/NGYS; 115 (Background), Photodisc; 115, Nick Upton/MP; 116 (Background), Triff/SS; 116–117, Sachin Kalbag/NGYS; 116 (LOLE), ku za/NGYS; 116 (LORT), Decha Thapanya/SS; 117 (UP), harshal mehta/NGYS; 117 (LOLE), Arvind Balaraman/NGYS; 117 (LORT), Tracy Olive/NGYS; 118 (Background), Visun Khankasem/SS; 119–119, Wael Eldeep/ NGYS; 119 (INSET), David Littschwager/NGS; 120, Arvin Pierce/ NGYS; 121 (Background), iSIRIPONG/SS; 121, Flickr RF/Getty Images; 122 (Background), Jakkrit Orrasri/SS; 122, WOLF AVNI/ SS; 123, Joel Sartore/NGS; 124, Anthony Smith; 125 (Background), Photodisc; 125, Hideta Nagai/NGYS; 126 (Background), Photodisc; 126, Oleg Golovnev/SS; 127, Premaphotos/Alamy; 128, Dwight R. Kuhn; 129 (Background), Photodisc; 129, Kaldari/WK; 130 (Background), Visun Khankasem/SS; 130–131, chinahbzyg/SS; 131 (INSET), pixelman/ SS; **COMPLETE METAMORPHOSIS:** 132–133, Laitche/WK; 132 (UPLE), Leigh Ayres/NGYS; 132 (UPRT), smuay/SS; 132 (CTR), kurt_G/SS; 132 (LO), Peeravit/SS; 133, Eric Isselée/SS; 134–135, Yohan Yeo/NGYS; 135 (LOLE), Mike Quinn; 135 (LOCTR), Luca Barovier/NGYS; 135 (LORT), WK; 136 (Background), Photodisc; 136, Keith Thomson/NGYS; 137, mehmet karaca/NGYS; 137 (INSET), Laura Lopez/NGYS; 138, Hendroh/SS; 139 (UP), Pan Xunbin/SS; 139 (LO), Henrik Larsson/SS; 140–141 (Background), Triff/SS; 140–141, Mark Moffett/MP; 140 (LOLE), Chris Helliwell/ NGYS; 140 (LORT), kurt_G/SS; 141 (UP), Dr. Morley Read/SS; 141 (LORT), Paul Zahl/NGS; 141 (LOLE), David Littschwager/NGS; 142 (BACK), Visun Khankasem/SS; 142, Ch›ien Lee/MP; 143, Ch›ien Lee/MP; 144, Satoshi Kuribayashi/Nature Production/MP; 145 (Background), iSIRIPONG/SS; 145, Stephen Dalton/naturepl.com; 146 (UP), Radim Schreiber/NGYS; 146, Yonhap, Choi Byung-kil/ AP Images; 147, Radim Schreiber/NGYS; 148, Piotr Naskrecki/ MP; 150 (Background), lchumpitaz/SS; 150, Kenneth Garrett/ NGS; 151, Joel Sartore/NGS; 152, Nigel Cattlin/Visuals Unlimited/ Getty Images; 153 (Background), Visun Khankasem/SS; 153, Robert Harding World Imagery/Getty Images; 154 (Background), Jakkrit Orrasri/SS; 154, David Litschwager/NGS; 155, Paul Zahl/ NGS; 156, Margo Dollan/NGYS; 157 (Background), Photodisc; 157, Bruce MacQueen/SS; 157 (LO), Crystal Ernst; 158–159, john t. fowler/Alamy; 159 (INSET), Joel Sartore/NGS; 160, Wayne Bakker/NGYS; 161 (Background), iSIRIPONG/SS; 161, David Littschwager/NGS; 161 (Background), Photodisc; 162–163, Muhammad Mahdi Karim/WK; 163 (INSET), Michael & Patricia Fogden/MP; 164, Thomas Marent/MP; 165, Satoshi Kuribayashi/ Nature Production/MP; 166–167 (Background), Triff/SS; 166–167, Scott Frazier/NGYS; 166 (LOLE), Pan Xunbin/SS; 166 (LORT), kurt_G/SS; 167 (UP), Darwin Lucena/NGYS; 167 (LOLE), Nicky Bay/NGYS; 167 (LORT), Darlyne A. Murawski/NGS; 168, Garrett Hargiss/NGYS; 169 (Background), Visun Khankasem/SS; 169, Dehaan/WK; 170 (Background), iSIRIPONG/SS; 170–171, tamara kavalou/NGYS; 171 (INSET left), Frank Hecker; 171 (INSET right), errni/SS; 172–173, Luis Miguel Bugallo Sánchez/WK; 174, Paul Pomeroy/NGYS; 175, samantha schwann/NGYS; 176–177, Kristy Potter/NGYS; 177, jen king/NGYS; 178–179, J. Rowan/Photri Images/Alamy; 179, Rob Carr/AP Images; 180, Aynia Brennan/ NGYS; 181 (Background), Visun Khankasem/SS; 181, Steve Irvine/ NGYS; 182–183, Richard Becker/FLPA; 182 (INSET), Victorian Traditions/SS; 183 (INSET), Photo Fun/SS; 184–185, George Grall/ NGS; 186–187, A.N.T. Photo Library/NHPA/Photoshot; 186 (LOLE), Konrad Wothe/MP; 186 (LORT), Jonathan Garcia/NGYS; 186–187, Triff/SS; 187 (UP), lisa mowry/NGYS; 187 (LOLE), Jonathan Wright/NGYS; 187 (LORT), chuck spencer/NGYS; 188–189, Stewart Marsden/NGYS; 188 (INSET), Chris Kidd/NGYS; 189 (INSET), Heidi Andrade/NGYS; 190–191, Jef Meul/Foto Natura/MP; 191, MarkMirror/SS; 192 (Background), Jakkrit Orrasri/SS; 192–193, Colin Ewington/Alamy; 193 (INSET), karthi keyan/NGYS; 194, Robert Sisson/NGS; 195 (INSET), Alex Wild/ Visuals Unlimited, Inc./Getty Images; 196 (INSET), Mark Moffett/ NGS; 196 (INSET lo), Darlyne A. Murawski/NGS; 196–197, Ramesh Thanapandi/NGYS; 198, James P. Blair/NGS; 198 (INSET), Mark W. Moffett/NGS; 199 (Background), Photodisc; 199 (INSET), Peter Essick/NGS; 200 (Background), Photodisc; 200, Stephen Dalton/MP; 201, Darlyne A. Murawski/NGS; 202, Jaime Gadala Maria/NGYS; 203 (INSET up), johan botes/NGYS; 203 (LO), Marius Jursys/NGYS; 204 (Background), Photodisc; 204, David Littschwager/NGS; 205, Robin Loznak/NGYS; 206–207, Paul Zahl/ NGS; 207, sumita roy/NGYS; 208 (Background), Jakkrit Orrasri/ SS; 208, Daniel Feliciano/WK; 209, Alvesgaspar/WK; 210–211, Laurie Campbell/naturepl.com; 211 (INSET), David Littschwager/ NGS; 212 (BACK), Photodisc; 212, Francesco Brazzelli/NGYS; 213, Muhammad Mahdi Karim/WK; 214, Dr. Alice Wells/Australian National Insect Collection/Australian National Wildlife Collection/ CSIRO Ecosystem Sciences; 215 (BACK), Visun Khankasem/SS; 215, Picavet/Workbook Stock/Getty Images; 216 (Background), Digital Stock; 216, Arnaldo Ronca/NGYS; 217, Renant Cheng/ NGYS; 218 (INSET), Jason Patrick Ross/SS; 218, Cathy Keifer/SS; 219 (Background), Photodisc; 219 (INSET), April Moore/NGYS; 220–221, Greg Hume/WK; 221 (INSET), Cheryl McMahan/NGYS; 222, Florian Andronache/SS; 223 (Background), Photodisc; 223, Darlyne A. Murawski/NGS; 224 (Background), Photodisc; 224, Robert Clark/NGS; 225, Natasha Drouin/NGYS; 226, Edward Mattis/NGYS; 227 (Background), Photodisc; 227, Susan DeCosta/ NGYS; 228 (Background), Jakkrit Orrasri/SS; 228, Maksimilian/ SS; 229, Belozorova Elena/SS; 230, Faizan Khan/NGYS; 231 (Background), Visun Khankasem/SS; 231, Joel Sartore/NGS; 232–233 (Background), Triff/SS; 232–233, Rowland Cole/NGYS; 232 (LOLE), johnbraid/SS; 232 (LORT), Nikos Tsatsakis/NGYS; 233 (UP), Richard L B Ong/NGYS; 233 (LOLE), Phil Thorogood/NGYS; 233 (LORT), M. Williams Woodbridge/NGS; 234–235, Karolos Trivizas/NGYS; 235 (Background), Photodisc; 235 (INSET), paul coleman/NGYS; 236 (Background), Photodisc; 236–237, Ingo Arndt/Foto Natura/MP; 237 (INSET), Kulac/WK; 238, Alexander Humphreys/NGYS; 239 (Background), Digital Stock; 239, Reuters; 240 (Background), Photodisc; 240 (INSET), Peter Zagar/NGYS; 241, Mitsuhiko Imamori/MP; 241 (INSET), Mitsuhiko Imamori/ MP; 242, Roy Toft/NGS; 243 (Background), Photodisc; 244 (Background), iSIRIPONG/SS; 244, Esc861/WK; 245, Melinda Fawver/SS; 245 (INSET), Edward Brubaker/iStockphoto; 246, Dr. Hans Banziger; 247 (Background), Jakkrit Orrasri/SS; 247, Dr. Hans Banziger; **BACK MATTER:** 248–249, jps/SS; 248 (UP), Doug Lemke/SS; 248 (LOLE), Vladimir Kim/SS; 248 (LORT), Mirvav/SS; 249 (UP), Lewis Scharpf/NGYS; 249 (LO), Lukas Jonaitis/NGYS; 250–251 (Background), Photodisc; 250 (UP), courtesy Bill Lamp; 250 (LO), John Davidson; 251 (UPLE), Bob Jensen/Collection/ Photoshot; 251 (LO), Wael Eldeep/NGYS; 251 (UPRT), eric wright/ NGYS; 252 (CTR), Dave Bevan/Alamy; 252 (RT), SS; 252–253 (Background), Photodisc; 253, Grtechen Stuppy Carlson/; 254–255, karthi keyan/NGYS; 254 (UP), Helene Schmitz/NGS; 254 (LO), Chris Minihane/NGYS; 255 (LOLE), Heather Davis/NGYS; 255 (LORT), Cathy Keifer/SS; 255 (UP), Darlyne A. Murawski/NGS; 256–257 (Background), Photodisc; 256–257, SDeming/SS; 257, Jonathan Lewis/Oxford Scientific RM/Getty Images; 258–259 (Background), Triff/SS; 258, Jurgen Otto; 258 (LOLE), Julius Cesar Garcia/NGYS; 258 (UPLE), Yudha Pratama/NGYS; 258 (LORT), Yudha Pratama/SS; 259 (UPLE), Gerry Ellis/Digital Vision; 259 (UPRT), Arnold Koenig/NGYS; 259 (LO), Gowtham Shankara/ NGYS; 260 (UPLE), Radim Schreiber/NGYS; 260 (LOLE), Heidi Andrade/NGYS; 260–261 (Background), Visun Khankasem/SS; 260 (RT), Pan Xunbin/SS; 261 (LE), Jacob Benner-Tufts University/Reuters; 261 (RT), Vilainecrevette/SS; 262–263 (Background), Visun Khankasem/SS; 262 (LE), Mladen Bozickovic/NGYS; 262 (RT), Jessica Straw/NGYS; 263 (UP), Kristina Postnikova/SS; 263 (CTR), Amir Ridhwan/SS; 263 (LO), Mitsuhiko Imamori/MP; 264–265, Digital Stock; 264 (UPLE), mehmet karaca/NGYS; 264 (UPRT), irin-k/SS; 264 (CTR), Chris Kidd/NGYS; 264 (LORT), Premkumar Antony/NGYS; 264 (LOLE), Scott Frazier/NGYS; 265 (UPLE), Rowland Cole/NGYS; 265 (UPRT), bernadi gunawan/NGYS; 265 (LO), Paul Pomeroy/NGYS; 266–267 (Background), Phil Thorogood/NGYS; 268–269 (Background), Phil Thorogood/NGYS; 269 (Background), Photodisc; 271 (Background), Photodisc

Published by the National Geographic Society

John M. Fahey, *Chairman of the Board and Chief Executive Officer*
Declan Moore, *Executive Vice President; President, Publishing and Travel*
Melina Gerosa Bellows, *Executive Vice President; Chief Creative Officer, Books, Kids, and Family*

Prepared by the Book Division

Hector Sierra, *Senior Vice President and General Manager*
Nancy Laties Feresten, *Senior Vice President, Kids Publishing and Media*
Jay Sumner, *Director of Photography, Children's Publishing*
Jennifer Emmett, *Vice President, Editorial Director, Children's Books*
Eva Absher-Schantz, *Design Director, Kids Publishing and Media*
R. Gary Colbert, *Production Director*
Jennifer A. Thornton, *Director of Managing Editorial*

Staff for This Book

Priyanka Lamichhane, *Project Editor*
Susan Bishansky, *Project Manager*
Eva Absher-Schantz, *Art Director*
Lori Epstein, *Senior Photo Editor*
Ruthie Thompson, *Designer*
Christina Wilsdon, *Researcher and Fact-checker*
Ariane Szu-Tu, *Editorial Assistant*
Callie Broaddus, *Design Production Assistant*
Hillary Moloney, *Associate Photo Editor*
Carl Mehler, *Director of Maps*
Sven M. Dolling, *Map Research and Production*
Grace Hill, *Associate Managing Editor*
Joan Gossett, *Production Editor*
Lewis R. Bassford, *Production Manager*
Susan Borke, *Legal and Business Affairs*
Cathleen Carey, Moriah Petty, Jennifer Raichek, *Interns*

Production Services

Phillip L. Schlosser, *Senior Vice President*
Chris Brown, *Vice President, NG Book Manufacturing*
George Bounelis, *Vice President, Production Services*
Nicole Elliott, *Manager*
Rachel Faulise, *Manager*
Robert L. Barr, *Manager*

I thank my wife and family for their continuing love and support, and my students, colleagues, and teachers who kept me engaged with the world of insects.
—Bill Lamp

To Luis Carlos, Bruce, and all bug lovers.
—Darlyne Murawski

For my brother, Kevin. I hope this makes up for the yellow-jacket incident.
—Nancy Honovich

CELEBRATING 125 YEARS

The National Geographic Society is one of the world's largest nonprofit scientific and educational organizations. Founded in 1888 to "increase and diffuse geographic knowledge," the Society's mission is to inspire people to care about the planet. It reaches more than 400 million people worldwide each month through its official journal, *National Geographic,* and other magazines; National Geographic Channel; television documentaries; music; radio; films; books; DVDs; maps; exhibitions; live events; school publishing programs; interactive media; and merchandise. National Geographic has funded more than 10,000 scientific research, conservation, and exploration projects and supports an education program promoting geographic literacy.

For more information, please visit www.nationalgeographic.com, call 1-800-NGS LINE (647-5463), or write to the following address:
National Geographic Society
1145 17th Street N.W.
Washington, D.C. 20036-4688 U.S.A.

Visit us online at www.nationalgeographic.com/books

For librarians and teachers: www.ngchildrensbooks.org

More for kids from National Geographic:
kids.nationalgeographic.com

For information about special discounts for bulk purchases, please contact National Geographic Books Special Sales: ngspecsales@ngs.org

For rights or permissions inquiries, please contact National Geographic Books Subsidiary Rights: ngbookrights@ngs.org

Hardcover ISBN: 978-1-4263-1376-9
Library edition ISBN: 978-1-4263-1377-6

Printed in the United States of America

13/CK-CML/1